Alpine Climbing

ALPINE CLIMBING

John Barry

The Crowood Press

First published in 1988 by
The Crowood Press
Ramsbury
Marlborough
Wiltshire
SN8 2HE

British Library Cataloguing in Publication Data

Barry, John, *1944 –*
    Alpine climbing.
    1. Mountaineering – Manuals
    I. Title
    796.5′ 22

ISBN 1 85223 001 0

Typeset by Action Typesetting Limited, Gloucester
Printed in Great Britain at the University Printing House, Oxford

DEDICATION

To the unknown father and unknown son who came to the Alps on yon tiny motorbike and climbed their mountains without fuss. They'll have advanced well beyond the scan of this book by now, but it is for them anyhow.

And it is also, if I am allowed, for this Alaskan lady:

That night there was a party. A friendly lady from a local radio station addressed me, half small-talk, half interview, 'Say, why you guys in Alaska?'

'We're going climbing.'

'Mountains?'

'Yeah, Deborah.'

'Ain't never heard of no Deborah, but I went up a mountain one time, an' when I was 'bout half way up, I looked up, an' I looked down, an' I said, Lady, there ain't nothin' I need up there, so I went back down.'

I thought her very sane; I still do.

ACKNOWLEDGEMENTS

The section on lightning is reproduced by kind permission of the Scottish Sports Council, from Eric Langmuir's *Mountain-craft and Leadership* published jointly by the Scottish Sports Council and the Mountain Walking Leader Training Board (second edition 1984).

My thanks are also due to the following: Mike Woolridge and Nicky Wright for all the diagrams and for cheerfully accommodating my every whim and amendment; Pat Littlejohn and John Brailsford for photographs; Malcolm Campbell, John Cousins, Nigel Shepherd, Mike Woolridge (again), Jeff Lowe and The Swiss National Tourist Office for unstinting advice and unrewarded assistance of one form or another; Kath and Dotti for typing through the nights; and all my alpine partners over the years, perhaps DVN especially, for a hundred great alps.

Contents

Alpinism

THE NATURE OF THE GAME

Alpinism: it is perhaps a useful thing to define the activity. Alpinism is one of those games that climbers play usually, though by no means necessarily, after they have already played at rock climbing and, perhaps, at ice climbing too. That is the traditional order of things and though it doesn't have to be conducted in that order, first-year alpine aspirants will have a better time of it if they can already climb on rock and ice to some degree. But as I say, it doesn't have to be that way – hill walkers can play the game too.

Fig 1   The Matterhorn, quintessential alp.

Alpinism is much more than the game that follows ice climbing – though it is often that; much more than the sum of rock and ice climbing – though it is certainly that; much more than views and vistas – though there are those in plenty; and more yet than that mountaineering which happens in alpine regions. The alpine game will not be so easily sited; by its breadth it resists definition, by its variety, package; by its diversity, category. Yet I must try to define it, if only to tell you what this book attempts.

Alpinism, then, is that game we play in the alps, any alps, which these days range from altitudes of 5,000 to nearly 30,000 feet. It is a game of climbing among mountains, or on them – and usually, but not always, nor necessarily, to the top of them. It is a game played on rock, sometimes only on rock; a game played on ice, sometimes exclusively on ice; and it is a game played on both, alternately as well as at once – yes, even with one foot on each of those things at the same time – and on every infinite variety, mixture or conglomeration of snow, ice, rock, earth and dust.

It is a game, traditionally played in alpine playgrounds, the European Alps, the Southern Alps of New Zealand and the Cascades or Rockies of North America, for example, that is now carried to farther flung pitches – to Alaska, the Karakoram, the Himalayas, and the Arctic and Antarctic. Indeed the alpine writ now runs fairly large anywhere on the earth's mountainous surface. And the game travels well, to the highest mountains, K2 and Everest, as well to more modest, if more technical, altitudes.

But even as the alpine game advances into the greater ranges, so it has shrunk away a bit at the other end, the traditional end of alpinism, allowing the pure rock climbing game and the pure ice climbing game to win inroads. By that I mean that climbers are treating bits of alps as crags, and not much more than roadside crags at that. And because they are treated as crags, they are climbed in shorts, and T-shirt and chalkbag and abseiled down before any summit is seen, in time for tea. And bravo. Or in winter, today's ice climber might ski in a minute and a swoop to some lonely couloir, subdue it at a trot, abseil down the same ice and ski to a beer. Again bravo. But are these things alpinism? Certainly they have occured in alps, certainly it is climbing – but alpinism? I just don't know. And although I don't really care either – for what does it matter? – it's fun to conject and it is never, surely, a bad thing trying to define the indefinable.

Now every time I think of a factor that is exclusively alpine, soon after another thought unearths an exception. Glaciers: I thought that was a safe one. Alpinism always involves glaciers whereas, say, Ben Nevis, otherwise as fit to be an alp as any Eiger, is approached by a bog (would that it *was* a glacier). So there indeed is the essential difference between the Super Couloir and Point Five Gully. But the North Face of the Eiger itself rises straight from the train, and a meadow full of cows and buttercups – and who'd have said that the games played on that face were not alpinism? Altitude then. But that's not much good as a specifying factor either. The Lyngen Alps in Arctic Norway, are only 5,000 feet high (and though rising from the sea, are riven with glaciers), whereas the highest summits on every continent are now (sometimes) climbed as if they were alps. Weather: well there's not much to choose between a Cairngorm tempest, an Alaskan howler or a Himalayan storm. No future in that line of argument.

At the end I'll settle for a compromise: the alpinism of this book is a game played on mountains of snow or ice or rock, more usually on glaciated ground, more often at altitudes of 10–20,000 feet, as a rule starting somewhere near the mountain's natural bottom and going on to a natural top, and involving the full array of mountaineering skills and . . . and all the rest – all those other things, other places, anything you want it to be, anywhere. Those general precepts that can be applied to any hills – or discarded at will; tools for fun, to be dropped when they no longer work or amuse; diversions for diversion, to be thrown down when the sun's rays make you bring out your rock boots, shorts and chalkbag, or when the actual summit's an easy mile away and the way down is the other way; a game to play as hard as you like – but not much more than a game after all. For all that though, it's a good game; maybe a great one.

This explanation of that game is for beginners – first or second timers; beyond that you'll be making your own plays. My aim is to supply sufficient knowledge to begin in decent safety – for those who want to begin that way. This book is for first steps only. A book, any book, can only teach so much: the greater teacher is Experience. I hope this book will be useful as well as entertaining, but the required reading, the absolutely essential reading, will not be found in its pages – nor in those of any other manual. It is to be found only out on the mountains. You write it yourself with your own experiences, your own adventures. However, knowledge gleaned from within these covers should better prepare you to make the most of that experience, better equip you to reap reward from the adventure. 'True satisfaction is not to be found in courting unknown dangers for which you are ill-prepared, but in matching your own skill and experience against danger and difficulties of which you are aware.'

Read this book, or any of its sections, a dozen times, and you will still not be a master of the game; but you will be master of the first step. After that, your guides must be a judicious mixture, for which there is no fixed recipe, of ambition, ability and experience – though you can always return to the book to refresh, relearn, or to read on. I hope it accompanies you on as many steps as you have the inclination to take.

A note: throughout this book I will incline to one alpine region more than others; I'll lean to Europe. There are good and not so good reasons. A good reason is that historically the European Alps is where the game started and where, therefore, its traditions – those, that is, that survive – were founded. A not so good reason is that, although I have climbed Alps from New Zealand to the Himalayas to Norway to Alaska, by far the greater part of my experience has been won (and lost) in the Alps of France, Switzerland and Italy. But it matters hardly at all: the game is truly international and is played with the same shaped ball on every nation's alpine pitch.

1 Introducing the Alps

Throughout this book I have generally assumed that the reader has already some knowledge and experience of rock climbing and of climbing on snow and ice, so I'm also assuming that you know about knots and harness and tying on; about runners and belays; about axes and crampons and all the other paraphernalia of ice – for all those things and skills and practices are common to climbing in the alps. However, there are dozens of classic alpine ascents – including that of Mont Blanc itself – that can be safely undertaken by vigorous hill walkers who have reinforced their lowland hill skills with nothing more than the most basic of alpine skills, such as self arrest, walking in crampons and roped movement over glaciers. And I have tried to cater for these folk, whose sights are set commendably and literally high, but whose aim is too often deflected by unnecessary jargon of obfuscating technicality, by including a section on basic axe and crampon skills – this notwithstanding my earlier averral that this book is aimed at those who can already climb on snow and rock at some level. No, a

Fig 2   Glaciers of 'labyrinthian complexity': the Godwin-Austen Glacier at the foot of the Abruzzi Spur on K2, the world's second mightiest alp!

second thought says that alps can be for everyone. So I have included sections for those wishing to make the transition from hill walking to walking amongst, and over, alps.

Despite anything I may have said in my preamble, it's worth looking at what it is that makes alpine climbing different, that makes it special. Most of the alpine peak of Europe lie between 9,000ft and 15,000ft whilst alps of other regions may rise to 20,000ft (I'm talking averages; generalities). Mt. Kenya, for example, is 17,085ft (5199m); Mt Huntington, a fine Alaskan Alp, is 12,240ft (3721m); while the Alps of Peru, the Cordillera Blanca, lie between 16,000ft and 22,000ft. General conditions at any of these altitudes are more serious than in non-alpine regions. There are glaciers, often of labyrinthian complexity, and ice-falls and crevasses; there's snow, often metres deep, and ice often thousands of metres long; there are avalanches and stonefall; there are storms more cataclysmic, more sudden, than those on lower, gentler hills; there are days and distances that are longer, more arduous; and climbs that may be measured in days and thousands of metres rather than in hours and hundreds of feet – which might be the case nearer to home. There is a paradox here: alpine ascents are getting shorter – Christopher Prophit's ascent of the North faces of the Matterhorn, the Eiger and the Walker Spur in 24 hours, for example – while rock climbing on roadside crags has attained such a stretch of gymnastic improbability that the ascent of ten feet of

Fig 3   Dave Nicholls gives a crevasse a narrower berth than he might!

Fig 4 'There are days and distances that are longer': the West Ridge of the S. Summit of Gauri Sankar, Nepal (7,000m). This ridge, which consumed 23 days of continuous climbing, is over 4km long.

rock, with the rehearsing and linking of the necessary upward moves (never mind those downward) might consume two or three days – 27 days for a 40 foot gritstone problem gained was a recently recorded case.

There are other differences. Most alpine routes, even the simplest and easiest, will involve two stages and consume two or more days. Stage one, day one: getting to a hut (or in the US, more commonly a high camp) from which to begin the climb; stage two, day two (and maybe days three or four): the climb itself. Even then there may be a lengthy descent to regain the hut or valley, or to gain a different hut or valley,

and then again the return to your campsite. Speed is a virtue. Two minutes or two hours or two days on a crag matters little – except that your partner might be bored to narcolepsy – but time spent on an alp is maybe time between two storms and to dwell is to risk a change in the weather. In these circumstances virtuous speed may triumph over fragile ethics (or pedantic principle) so that a pull-on or a stand-in a sling will be the better solution to a difficult move than a dozen rehearsals. Even today, when commendable crag ethics are being applied to more and more alpine rock, it is difficult to imagine a leader enduring twenty falls and then, if still failing, abseiling off rather than pulling on a peg on, say, the Exit Cracks, 5,000ft up the North Face of the Eiger. To spend time here may be to spend your last time. Mind you, you can do that if you want but I don't know anyone with principles that strong – happily.

In the alps accidents also assume a greater seriousness – a rescue from some remote alpine face is no light thing, – though high-flying, powerful, modern helicopters have softened the business, once they know you're there. Then there's altitude too. Few of us perform as well at 14,000ft as we do at 400ft. A hand jam at altitude is a markedly more tiring device than one on a Derbyshire gritstone edge and a strenuous sequence of jams may exhaust lungs before arms. Nor is climbing a rope's length on 50 degree ice the soul-satisfying cruise that it might be at sea-level for the lungs may run out long before the rope. No, the alps can be hard work – though it gets easier as you gain fitness and acclimatisation.

But don't be discouraged. Alpine climbing is a magnificent game: perhaps the aristocrat of all the games that climbers play. I remember my own impressions at my first full alpine game, on Mt. Cook of the Southern Alps of New Zealand as it happened.

'It was late when we reached the Plateau Hut and we were tired, but not so tired that we couldn't sit on the roof and stare with wonder at what we beheld. Here were mountains, real ones, Mt. Cook, a huge bulk, sovereign and mighty; Mt. Tasman, a symmetry of graceful sweeps of snow, more beautiful than I imagined a mountain could be; and Silberhorn, Teichelmann, Dampier, each a shining star that cluttered the kaleidoscope of our vision, each a chord resounding in the clamour of our thought. We may not have come on to that plateau on "soft foot, breath held like a cap in the hand", we may have been unlovely boors in the valley, but we qualified for a seat on that roof by our hearts; they were in exactly the right place and we – we were in love. In love with it all.

'Spellbound. For a long while no one spoke. We gazed, dreamed, gaze on dream, dream on gaze. Our fancies, flighted free, fled ridges, flew crests, up, up to dwell on summits. Then they tumbled, gaze and dream and flight and fancy, one upon the other and we were lost in the joyous welter of it all. Silence... '

AN ALPINIST'S SKILLS

Good alpinists are many things. They'll be fit and hardy, weatherwise (and nearly weatherproof), good judges of conditions, planners as well as improvisors; route finders, avoiders of unnecessary toil and unwanted crevasses, and above all, but in addition to all, good all-round climbers, equally at home on rock or ice or mixed. A more detailed look at these things forms the substance of this book.

Fitness

A Scottish winter day is generally agreed to be a fairly arduous one. An alpine day – again I'm talking averages – is generally considered to be more arduous, by a bit at least.

The first routes always seem to be hard work as the muscles strain to accommodate greater loads and distances and gains in height, and as the blood and lungs take time to acclimatise and accustom, but, by the third route you'll be getting all-round fit and pleasure will be overtaking pain. Be kind to yourself though, and go fit in the first place. Long walks in any hills, or climbing on remote hard-to-get-to crags or longish jogs, are all ways to get in shape.

Technical fitness is important too. The White Spider is not the place to perfect your front-pointing, nor is the West Face of the Dru the best place to hone your hand jamming. It is wise to serve an apprenticeship at home before venturing on to bigger hills. 50 metres on the Brenva ridge will cost the lungs more than 50 metres on Tower Ridge, though the latter is technically harder; and 50 metres of alpine rock at grade IV will, to begin with at any rate, feel stiffer than your local Severe (5.5/5.6), even though technically they are about the same. Boots and rucksacks and altitude – and maybe tiredness and heat and thirst – will exact a toll until acclimatised and experienced.

Rock Climbing

In theory, and in fact in practice, if you can rock climb at home you can rock climb in the alps. Movement up and over rock, types of holds and use of those holds are identical and need no modification except that it is a good thing to get into the habit of doing it all more quickly – which may mean adopting those alpine ethics like pulling on slings, standing in them, using nuts and pegs for direct aid, standing on your second's shoulders or head, or whatever expediency prevails over principle in the circumstances. Standard rope and runner and belaying techniques apply too though there are useful modifications, usually in the interests of alacrity, which are described on pages 149–159. Those whose rock climbing has hitherto been performed exclusively in

lightweight, sticky, rock shoes, and who have designs on mixed alpine routes where they'll necessarily wear boots, or on major alpine rock routes where they might wear heavier-than-usual boots, would do well to practice in that heavier footwear at home, so that the differences in performance and technique do not come as a great suprise – or disappointment.

Remember, that whereas on your local crags the great majority of your routes will lie on rock of the best quality, pitches on

Fig 5   The Albinoni/Gabarrou Couloir on Mont Blanc du Tacul at about 13,000 ft. Not the place to learn about front-pointing. Fig 184 shows the general whereabouts of this fine route.

alpine rock not infrequently lie on rock so poor as would be ignored elsewhere, rock with a distinctly temporary feeling.

Snow and Ice

Similarly, if you can climb the waterfall ice of your local winter playground or scramble happily up such as Tower Ridge on Ben Nevis, then you can climb the snow and ice of the alps. The same skills apply with almost no modification. Handwork with axe (or axes) and footwork, with or without crampons, is identical. What is different is the altitude (again), the fact that speed is virtuous (again), and that you'll be persuaded to move faster than you might at home, perhaps by dint of moving together on ground where, were speed less of a thing, you might traverse in pitches (*see* page 150). The trade-off between speed and security is a delicate negotiation and one which only experience will make easy.

It is, however, better to go to the alps with something more than simple proficiency in snow and ice skills. Better to be adept. There may be great snow-bound distances to be covered or heights to gain or lose and, as I have said, perhaps too often now, speed is of the essence; not that scurrying Scottish sprint for the last crest but a good steady, day-long, distance-gobbling, competence – sure-shod and sure-footed.

Remember too that even if your alpine heart is set exclusively on rough, red, sunny alpine rock it may be that your way to that rock lies across a glacier, or over snow or ice; or that the descent is snow-bound. Even for the purest-hearted rock climber some snow and ice experience is essential (though *see* Chapter 7). Not that it is ever too late; there are local snow and ice practice areas at

Fig 6   Dave Nicholls savours space and aura on the Traverse of the Gods, N. Face of the Eiger.

all alpine venues – '*écoles des glaces*' where the rock athlete can learn a useful thing or two, the snowman hone his skills yet sharper, and the all-round adept become all-round even more adept. A good way to spend a rest day or a day of middling weather perhaps – and a good time to practise getting yourself and your partner out of a crevasse (*see* p 134), something few first-season alpinists will have practised in advance (though rehearsals are perfectly possible).

WHERE AND HOW TO BEGIN

Happily, there are alps the world over. The chances are that you will begin in your nearest alpine range. For Europeans that is clearly the European Alps. My own first alps were those of New Zealand, which in 1969 were my closest, and for which I retain a warm affection – though some of my experiences there were much colder. But any alpine area will do so long as there are mountains and routes upon them to match your ability. There's no harm in aiming low for the first route. It will be invaluable experience at any grade and altitude and you can always climb harder and higher the next

time out – and there's a better chance there will be a next time out than if you start too hard or too high. Later in this chapter is an explanation of the various alpine gradings and technical comparisons used around the world, but again it is perhaps better not to attempt to transpose your best valley, rock or ice grade directly on to alps. Rather, give your body and mind time to acclimatise – exposure and space and aura sometimes take some getting used to.

Research your area well. Study maps and guide books so that you know it in advance, have a feel for it, are becoming familiar with it (*see* pages 18 and 19). Get to know which approaches service which huts and which huts service which mountains and, more

Fig 7 '*Which huts service which routes?*': *the Temple Ecrins Hut on the western approach to the Barre Des Ecrins. In the background (from left to right) rise Les Bans, Mount Gioberney and Pic du Says.*

intimately, which routes on those mountains. This general feel for an area is at least a useful thing; at most it could, in an emergency, be a life-saver.

Courses or Companions – Party Size

There are two popular ways of embarking on an alpine career. One is to go with a mate and, working together, make your own discoveries, and, feeling your way, learn as you go. In many ways this is the more satisfying approach and the lessons learned from mistakes (and there are bound to be some) will be well learned, whilst the lessons from epics (provided they are survived) will be indelibly chalked on your blackboard of experience. This way is also enormous fun, more than a little exciting and often a cementer of special and lasting friendships – the odd tiff along the way notwithstanding. If this is the approach you elect to pursue you need do nothing more than serve an apprenticeship on rock and then ideally but not necessarily, another on your winter playground, acquire some gear (*see* Chapter 2) a map and a guidebook, and go. The alps are your oysters.

However, perhaps a safer and maybe a surer way to learn is by attending a course run by some recognised training agency (*see* Appendices V and VI). Certainly this is the method preferred by all mothers of aspirant alpinists. Such a course, usually between one and two weeks long, will to some extent speed you through all those awkward first steps, see you painlessly to your first huts, safely across your first glaciers, surely up to your first summits and speedily back to the valley again. You'll be learning from climbers far more experienced than yourself and you'll be absorbing the technicalities more quickly because that's all you have to concern yourself with; all the other alpine nags – the weather, the way, the time – can be left to exercise your mentor's mind.

It will cost you of course, and you have to balance that cash against the cost of beginning the other way, which may be false trails followed, glacier gambles, failed routes and a host of other not necessarily entertaining epics. My head tells me that a training course is the best way to begin. My heart says, 'Do it with a mate'. 'You pays your money and takes your choice.' Some advise to begin with a mate who is more experienced than you, which seems sound advice so long as such a mate can be found, and once found, persuaded to take on an apprentice. Logically though, there must always be at least one hapless aspirant than whom no one is more experienced (and now, applying more recently conceived logic, it becomes clear that if every aspiring alpinist is chasing around for a more experienced partner then no one actually finds anyone to climb with!).

I have said *a* mate. That is because the most usual number of an alpine climbing team is two. There are no rules about that, however, and teams of three and four are not uncommon, while even bigger teams are not unknown. But two is the normal and probably the fastest unit.

Insurance

Few climbers operating domestically bother to take out an insurance – even if one exists. For alpine climbing, however, it is well worth the comparatively small investment. You may lose gear through theft (depressingly common in Europe), or through carelessness, or by an accident. Some of those losses may be expensive to make good. You might be unfortunate enough to need rescuing by helicopter. Uninsured that will be very expensive. Insured you can afford to enjoy the ride. And rescues may arise from bizarre circumstances. I know one young lad who was lying on the top of a wall outside a hut, basking in the twin heats of the sun and the aftermath of his first alpine route. He fell asleep, and whilst sleeping he was stung by a bee. He rolled off the wall, fell but a few feet, and broke a leg. The fastest, least painful way to treatment was by helicopter. Happily he was insured.

Many national alpine clubs (for example, Club Alpin Français or The Swiss Alpine Club) offer insurances for their members and it is certainly worth considering one of these schemes if you join a club. The British Mountaineering Council has organised an insurance scheme for mountaineers which is at least as good as those available through an insurance broker. Typical lengths of cover on offer vary from a fixed number of months in a year (based on an average alpine season), to a year-round accident policy, to a whole-life policy to cover you *inter alia* against climbing accidents anywhere in the world. Clearly the last arrangement is the most expensive. Policies may be for gear only, or for accident only, or, again at a price, for both.

In Europe, EEC regulations provide some help for citizens, but it is barely adequate. (Britons be sure to obtain a form E111 from your local DHSS office. Production of this form at a hospital will make things much easier and usually spare you from having to fork out there and then. Some insurance schemes are only valid if backed up by an E111.)

In the USA there are no such arrangements or rescue insurances. However, there is a long-standing tradition of volunteer rescue, so that virtually all rescue services are provided free of charge. Climbers insure against injury and equipment loss through their regular insurance firms.

Duration of Visit

To most, a European alpine season means three or four weeks, while four to six weeks is probably about average for farther flung alpine ranges such as Alaska, South America or the Himalayas. However, a lot can be achieved in two; indeed a keen team will often achieve as much in two weeks of charging as a sluggish team in six weeks of sloth. The problem with a two-week holiday is that a prolonged spell of bad weather can make a nasty hole in it, but if two weeks is all you have, go to it – urgency climbs many mountains, desire more yet. Stays of longer than six weeks have a tendency to degenerate into a counter-productive torpor, with the flesh and spirit chasing each other through the bright lights of Chamonix City or some such, so that there have been teams who went to the Alps for an entire summer, and who went hell-bent as lions to return hung-over lambs with tails between untested legs and no tales of endeavour that could not have fitted a single month.

GUIDEBOOKS AND MAPS

Most of the popular alpine climbing regions of the world are well documented as far as guidebooks are concerned. It is, of course, perfectly possible to climb in any alps without a guidebook, though such an approach seems to be unnecessarily cussed in an area such as the European Alps, where the use of one of a number of excellent guides will save many false starts, false trails, routes lost and summits missed – enhancing the adventure rather than detracting from it. However, if your own brand of adventure frowns on the use of guidebooks, no problem. There are many superb alpine areas where no guidebook exists in the first place – Kishtwar and Zanskar, two regions of the Indian Himalayas, for example. And there are other areas to which you'll be lucky to find a map. So there's plenty of scope for the wildest adventures even after you've exhausted the documented mountains.

Guidebooks will supply you with most, if not all, of the information that you'll need, especially when visiting an area for the first time: details of valley bases, access to mountains, huts, routes, maps, retreats, passes, sources of weather forecasts, information about rescue, and very possibly much more. Good guidebooks make good reading in any case and browsing in one on one of those rest days or at the hut the night before the climb will often furnish you with details that may turn out to be important, and which in any case will give you a better feel for the general area.

Maps

I would seldom venture on to a mountain without a map, especially in an area that I didn't know well. Few, I suggest, would disagree with me. If weight or space were

Fig 8   Better to weatherproof your map (A) than to shred it (B).

crucial I might trim that map to its barest essentials, but map there would be. It's a good thing to weatherproof it; a poly bag at least, or better, some adhesive seal.

Alpine regions of Europe, North America and New Zealand have been definitively surveyed and you should experience little difficulty in finding the right map at major outdoor equipment retailers either in your own country or in one of the valley bases of your climbing area. (*See* Appendix VII for some of what is available.) Other areas are sketchily mapped, or as yet unmapped, but since these are unlikely to be the hills of your first forays, they need not concern you for the moment.

The most useful scales are 1:50,000 or, for a more detailed look, 1:25,000. Remember to check the magnetic variation of your area before navigating with map and compass.

VALLEY BASES AND ACCOMMODATION

Every group of alps has its base or bases. Some acquire legendary status so that they become better known than the mountains that they serve – although the notion that a town ever served mountains is probably a new one to the student of human geography: distinctly a mountaineer's notion. But certainly bases and their mountains grow inseperable, even synonymous. Ask a young British alpinist where he's headed for the season and as like as not he'll answer 'Cham' (Chamonix), meaning that he is going to base himself in Cham and to climb the mountains of the Mont Blanc range, the Chamonix Aiguilles and all those delights. Seldom, if ever, will the reply be, 'The

Mont Blanc range'. Ask an ageing British alpinist the same question and he'll answer 'Cham', meaning Cham – or at least that tiny corner of it occupied by the Bar National.

Other famed valley bases and their mountains are Courmayeur with Mont Blanc (from the Italian side); Zermatt with the Eastern Pennines (the Matterhorn, Breithorn, Dent d'Herens etc.); Zinal with the Ober Gabelhorn and Rothorn; Promontogno with the Bregaglia (Piz Badile); Trento and Bolzano with the Dolomites; Ailefroide and La Berade with the Dauphiné. Farther afield, in Alaska, Talkeetna is linked with Mt. McKinley and the Alaska and Hayes ranges (although only by air); in Peru, the town of Huaraz is linked with the Cordillera Blanca; and in New Zealand, Mt. Cook village is linked with the Southern Alps and, of course, Mt. Cook itself. Guidebooks usually give details of appropriate valley bases and facilities on offer.

In most of these places, as in most other valley bases, you will have the choice between camping or staying at a bunk house or *pension*, or, and not for the indigent, a hotel. I'll discount the last since I've never met a climber rich enough – or at least not one who confessed to being rich enough – except perhaps in such places as Huaraz where these things are wonderfully inexpensive.

Camping is probably the most common form of valley accommodation. Europe is littered (though, happily, seldom literally) with good campsites which afford a patch of grass per tent (and not much more than that in Chamonix at the height of the season), lavatories and usually hot showers. All that and mountains and wine too. A climber needs little more. In short,

Fig 9   Valley base at La Berade, the Dauphiné.

European campsites are plentiful and well maintained, if crowded; perfect bases. It is sometimes possible to camp free 'à sauvage' that is, away from the recognised camping grounds. In most European countries this is discouraged, sometimes vigorously by the police, and in France it is frequently against local by-laws.

Take a big tent and some home comforts – a chair perhaps, or a pillow – you may, perforce, be confined to your tent for days on end by bad weather on the hill.

Wherever your base and whatever the local customs you'll pick up the lore soon enough; a native in no time.

Huts and Refuges

Some of the popular (and populated) Alpine regions of the world have a system of huts.

The European Alps is the classic example with a comprehensive chain, often two or three attendant on the same mountain – though from different sides, and varying in size from wooden or galvanised four-man bivouac boxes to full-scale mountain hotels. They are usually sited tactically to serve the most popular routes on a mountain and strategically to make them safe from avalanches and stonefall. Some European huts are as much as six hours walk from the valley: that can be quite a grind early in your holiday. Happily, most are closer to the road than that. Descriptions of huts and approaches are nearly always given in the appropriate guidebook and shown on most maps, and the way to them clearly marked on the ground with signposts and splashes of paint. Separate dormitories for the sexes are the exception rather than the rule and

21

the usual sleeping arrangements are room-wide bunks with ten or more to a bunk – 'commingling heat'! Eating habits vary nationally. The usual practice is to take up your own food, several days worth if you are intending a stay of that duration, and either:

1.   Cook it yourself on your own stove in an area or room designated to that purpose (a common practice in French huts), or outside if no place is provided.

2.   Give it to the guardian to cook it for you (the normal practice in Swiss huts, whose guardians seem to know by heart – or instinct – the precise cooking instructions for every evening meal on the planet, precooked, dehydrated or otherwise, not to mention an *haute cuisine* improvisation or two!).

3.   Another possibility is to buy meals at the hut. These are usually fairly expensive but often very good. Even if you do not wish to avail yourself of a cooked meal it is often possible to buy hot water by the jug or litre. This can be used to speed up your own food preparation or to reconstitute your entire meal and to brew hot (rather than boiling) tea. Using hot water provided by the hut in this way may save the weight of a stove and fuel on the walk in. Certainly, buying hot water at breakfast can save you a lot of time and fuss.

Some huts have no resident guardians. Here, clearly, you must prepare your own food. Your guidebook will explain the general practice of that area, and it is as well to know it before quitting the valley.

   The cost of staying at a hut can be reduced by joining the appropriate governing national organisation or by becoming a member of an Alpine club, such as the Austrian Alpine Club, The Alpine Club, or the BMC. In practice you would have to use a hut a lot to recoup the fee for joining the club in one season. There are good huts and bad and this depends not so much on the acrhitecture or position but on the warden and whether he or she is sociable and well disposed towards climbers (and whether the climbers are sociable and well disposed towards the hut warden). Some guardians are wonderful hosts, others ogres; a few are diehard anglophobes – even xenophobes perhaps – while at least one of my acquaintance (no happy meeting) detests all climbers with an equal and impartial intensity. One wonders if he's in the right job.

   Huts serving popular routes can be unbearably crowded mid-season or at weekends. Examples are the Gouter Hut on the Bosses Route on Mont Blanc, the Hornli Hut at the start of the easiest route up the Matterhorn, or the Ecrins Hut at the foot of the north side of the Barre des Ecrins in the Dauphiné. An overcrowded hut often means a poor night's rest and an utter chaos of stumbling, head-torched, gear-fumbling bodies in the morning – and morning starts any time after midnight. Such a night is a bad start to any alpine climb, and possibly terminal to your first. In such circumstances it may be better to consider bivouacking, even if that means a sack that is a few pounds heavier (*see* page 169). On the other hand some huts are absolute havens of stillness and calm and some wardens the very soul of charm and solicitude – the Les Bans Hut and Mimi the warden being particular favourites of mine.

   Guidebooks will nearly always indicate how long a particular hut approach will take (30 minutes to 6 hours is the European alpine bracket). These indicated times are averages. If you are much slower than the suggested time you should ask yourself why, and possibly trim your climbing plans to begin on something easier than you had intended. By the end of an alpine holiday you should be able to gain the huts comfortably within the time given in the guide. On the longer holiday, if you begin to slow again, it's probably time you went home – or avoided the bright lights and night spots. To be late to a hut is sometimes to incur more than just the inconvenience of being last and having to sleep on the floor or, in the worst case, being turned away altogether, for some huts are perched on improbable pinnacles and in the dark the last part of the path may be a disconcerting, or even dangerous, scramble.

A way to reduce, sometimes to avoid altogether, the labour of a hut approach is to use a *télépherique*, cable car or train – if one exists. Purists may gainsay me but I've yet to meet the man who can say nay to all of the variety of mechanisms that transform the Hornli Hut approach from at least six hours of purgatory to about two of pleasure – and if such a person exists, then I don't want to hear from him.

By whatever means you reach a hut and in whatever condition, remember to check-in with the guardian who will allot you a sleeping space – often with others who have your route or planned start time in common – tell you what the weather is doing, enquire whether you wish an evening meal or a breakfast, and perhaps a dozen other little things. Try to keep him sweet; don't wear clumpen boots in his front room – nearly all huts supply hut slippers and a rack for the stowing of boots;

Fig 10   The Bertol Hut, perched above Arolla, Switzerland , and home of Jean, surely the friendliest guardian in the alps.

don't leave your sack, axes and crampons around interiors – similar racks usually exist for axes and crampons, while in some huts sacks are forbidden beyond the porch. Then the sack should be left in the entrance and use made of one of the baskets that are nearly always provided to carry essentials within. Whenever possible settle your bill before going to bed – that's one less thing to think about in the morning.

Keep tabs on your gear, in the early morning scramble it is all too easy for someone to mistakenly take your axe – especially if it is a better model than their own – and it is not unknown for boots to walk away on the wrong feet. Being well organised saves time, energy and patience too; few things test the sang-froid quite as sorely as the multinational *brouhaha* of a full-scale Grand-Prix alpine start!

One last tip: time spent in reconnaissance is seldom wasted. Try to arrive at your hut with time enough to spy out the way to tomorrow's climb – it may save you hours, or even the climb itself. Points to look for are:

1.   The way out of the hut to the *beginning* of your approach to the route. This is not always straightforward. Huts are often sited at the top of quite steep slabs or pinnacles and the day's first steps may be climbing steps – or even an abseil.
2.   The best place to gain glacier or rock, as the case may be.
3.   Any paths or markers (cairns) or other features (for example, large boulders) that will help you along the right way in the pre-dawn dark. Whilst some huts may be quit at a carefree stroll, others must be left fully roped, cramponed and accoutred.

Note: Take your passport if your planned route takes you into a different country (for example, Switzerland to Italy over the Piz Badile).

Food

In the Valley

Make as big a pig of yourself as budget or vanity allows!

At the Hut

Weight is important, for unless you intend to eat hut fare (*see* page 22), you have to carry every gram every inch of the way – and that can be a long way. Basic local food is usually the cheapest and as good as anything you are likely to want to bring from home. Many survive very happily on bread – a *flute* atop a rucksack is considered *de rigueur* in the European Alps – cheese, salami, packet soups and tea or coffee. Others prefer a dehydrated meal or spagetti or macaroni though none of these cook very well at the highest huts because water boils at a lower temperature at altitude. Biscuits make good afters, especially if dunked in tea. Breakfast need be little more than a brew of tea or coffee and some cheese or salami again. The Scots will seldom go anywhere without porridge, which is good if you can be bothered, but messy if you can't. Muesli is an alternative.

On the Mountain

During the day, as you climb, or at rests, chocolate, sweets, biscuits, cheese, condensed milk from a tube, sugar lumps, dextrosol, and raisins all supply energy, conveniently and cleanly. Drink plenty of liquid. For bivouacs the same sort of food that you took to the huts will do admirably – perhaps complimented with some salt, if the route is to be a long one, to help in fending off cramp.

Liquid

In the valley, drink whatever takes your fancy. On the hill it is worth carrying a water bottle filled with water or orange juice or the like. Reconstituted powdered fruit drinks are especially refreshing. Thirst is very debilitating – drink as much as you feel you need, and be sure to fill your tank to overflowing in the hut or bivouac *before* the climb. A clever little ploy is to carry a short length of polythene straw or tube in your pocket so that whenever you see a trickle or a poolette of water you can suck it from otherwise inaccessible crannies, or nooks too tight for your nose, via the straw. But, whatever means you use to slake your thirst, remember, sufficient liquid is very important.

ACCLIMATISATION

Almost everyone can climb at European alpine altitudes with little more difficulty than perhaps some breathlessness at the hut on the first night (Cheyne-Stokes breathing as it is called), some hard panting on the hill the next day and maybe a headache. But none of these things, only mildly un-comfortable, is very much to worry about. It is probably best to aim for an alp of fairly modest altitude for your very first peak – say up to 12,500ft (3,800m). Very likely the worst thing that will happen at that height is that you'll puff a lot harder than at sea level, irrespective of your physical fitness. The next time at the height you'll go

noticeably better, and by about the third peak you'll be going like a train – that is if you are ever going to go like a train.

By all means go higher on your first route if you wish – nothing worse than headache and nausea will overtake you, and both will rapidly disappear once lower altitudes have been regained. Not everyone suffers equally. Indeed some people seem not to suffer at all. It's very unfair. They arrive in Chamonix a stone overweight and stroll straightway to the top of Mont Blanc. On the other hand I know a top-flight alpinist with some astonishing times to his credit who one season decided that the *voie normale* on Mont Blanc would be a very fine leg-stretch and warm-up for the greater things he had planned that season. In the event he stretched his lungs a lot further than his legs and that was a lot further than they wanted to be stretched. He failed to make the summit by several thousand feet returning to the valley with a sore head and a badly bruised ego – but nothing worse. Only a few weeks later in the same season he soloed the Droites by the North Face in less than four hours, a phenomenal time by any standards. By then he could have strolled up that *voie normale* in relative comfort. His mistake was to try to go too high on the first route of a season. I later saw him climb like a tiger at 22,000ft in the Himalayas, which rather reinforces the point.

In contrast, I know a girl who arrived in Chamonix from Britain one day, very fit but totally unacclimatised, and climbed the very next day to the top of Mont Blanc with no discomfort whatsoever. As I said, it isn't fair. But be consoled, given two or three weeks, and as many routes, almost everyone will be able to puff their way to Mont Blanc's summit (15,770ft, or 4,807m) or to that of any lesser alp. It's all a question of acclimatisation, of physiological adaption to the rarified air at these altitudes, and all that takes is a little time. Fitness, though unrelated to speed of acclimatisation, helps to make everything a little easier.

Further afield, on bigger hills, the process of acclimatisation is a much more serious and slower business altogether. If anyone was whisked from sea level to 23,000ft (7,000m) they would almost certainly die if they remained at that height. If your intended alp is 20,000ft (6,000m) high, say in Peru or the Himalayas, you should allow at least two weeks to reach the top, and three or even four would be better. To attempt to go above 23,000ft (7,000m) in less than four weeks is to invite altitude sickness.

Most people will experience some headaches and nausea whilst acclimatising to these sorts of altitudes. These will usually pass in a couple of days but if they persist then the only answer is to go down before a more serious problem such as oedema sets in. The specifics of acclimatising to super alpine altitudes are beyond the scope of this book but if you intend to climb on alps in excess of 5,000m you are strongly recommended to do some thorough homework in such books as *Medicine for Mountaineering* (Wilkerson) or *Mountain Sickness* (Hackett) (*see* Further Reading). Suffice it to say here that the well-established rules for going high and the not fully understood business of acclimatisation are:

1. Restrict your height gain to about 2,000ft (600m) a day. And if you have to climb higher than that by day, then arrange to sleep low.
2. Avoid strenuous exercise at altitude until you are fully acclimatised – usually a period of 3–4 weeks.
3. Drink plenty of fluid.

4. Lose height quickly, and then stay low for a couple of days, if you feel very ill.

A final point: the only time that I have ever suffered discomfort from altitude in the European alps has been when, immediately on arrival, I have taken a *télépherique* to a high place such as the Torino Hut above Courmayeur. Even then the trouble has been nothing more then a mild headache and some breathlessness. I have never suffered the slightest discomfort (at least not from altitude) when I have walked up from the valley floor, thereby gaining height much more slowly and more healthily. After a couple of routes it no longer seems to make any difference, and then *télépheriques* may be used to great advantage, saving time and labour without penalty other than financial.

GRADES AND STANDARDS

There are almost as many systems for grading alpine climbs, as there are nations with alps. For a beginner this can be a confusing, indeed a worrying, thing. At least all systems have one thing in common: they start at the easy end and work towards the wild side. In a way that is all that you need to know. A climb graded 1 will always be easier that one graded 6. Moreover, 1 is likely to be quite easy and, in a scale of 6, 6 is likely to be quite hard. Some systems run 1 to 6, or beyond; others use a combination of numbers and letters and still others use an adjectival system. If all this looks to be potentially confusing, don't worry. As I say the first point in the scale is always easy and the last, hard – those are really the only two absolutes.

Let's examine the system used in France

for its Alps. (They have a different system for their rock climbs, but it is still based on progressively hard gradations, 1–umpteen.) The French alpine system, sometimes called the Vallot system because it is employed by the Vallot series of guidebooks, is used by most British guidebook editors too. In this system the difficulty of the climb as a whole is assessed – based on average conditions and taking into account factors such as length, altitude, objective dangers (stone-fall, serac threat, etc), difficulty of route-finding, quality of rock and remoteness, as well as the technical difficulty of the climbing itself. Thus routes are given overall grades of:

Facile(F)	Easy
Peu Difficile(PD)	Not very hard
Assez Difficile(AD)	Fairly hard
Difficile(D)	Difficult
Très Difficile(TD)	Very difficult
Extremement Difficile(ED)	Extremely difficult

Where individual rock pitches warrant attention they are graded I–VI with *inférieur (inf)* and *supérieur (sup)* added as fine tuning where necessary: III *sup*, for example, is a little easier than IV *inf*. Very roughly, the traditional relationship between British and French rock is:

III	Very Difficult
IV	Severe, 4a
V	Very Severe, 4b – 4c
VI	Hard Very Severe, 5a

Artificial pitches, again traditionally – and I'll explain the significance of 'traditional' in a moment – are graded A1, A2, A3, A4, A5 in ascending difficulty.

Looking at the Vallot system more closely, on a mountain rock route graded *Difficile* you might expect to encounter a number of pitches of IV and maybe one or two of V. On a TD there would be numerous pitches of V, a few being V *sup* and maybe one or two of VI. A mixed route is graded according to general difficulty and may earn quite a high grade even though there is not a single gradeable rock pitch on it. The Swiss Route on the North Face of the Courtes at Chamonix, for example, is graded TD though there are no rock pitches on it. There is, however, some quite steep ice, which under the French system is not graded separately, but which would rate about 3 in Scotland, as well as lots of quite steep mixed ground.

Of the Swiss Route the Vallot guidebook says, '800m, TD, very beautiful... It is more difficult than the North Face of the Triolet with two extremely steep walls, one of two or three pitches in the bottom tier, the other of two pitches higher up.' So, apart from an overall TD, a mention of steep pitches – all ice, though now that I think about it the book doesn't say they're all ice – a useful comparison and some lyrical description, you're on your own as far as definitive technical information is concerned.

But French rock gradings on outcrops (some of them 600m high!) have recently been revised, and this revision has been adopted by many to fit to those mountain rock routes that are now frequently climbed as outcrops using outcrop ethics (discussed in Chapter 7). If you are going to treat alps as rock routes and not much more – which is fair enough – then it makes sense to judge them by rock climbing grades. This is what Michel Piola has done in his alpine rock guidebook series.

It's now worth reminding ourselves of how rock grades across the world compare:

Rock Grades Around the World

USA	Britain	France
3rd class		II
4th class		III
5.0 to 5.6	4a (Severe)	IV
5.7	4b, 4c (Hard Severe/VS)	IV & V
5.8	5a (HVS)	V
5.9	5b (E1)	V & VIa
5.10	5b (E1/E2)	VIb
	5c (E2/E3)	
5.11	6a (E3/E4)	VIc

It will be seen that while traditional French rock grades ran I–VI, they now run I–V with suffixes + or - (superior or inferior) and then VIa, VIb, VIc, VIIa and onwards in a theoretically open-ended system.

Let's take a route that has been, and still is, graded both ways: the American Direct on the Aiguille de Dru. Traditionally graded this is ED. In *The Alpine Club Guide*, Lindsay Griffin states, 'The route is normally completed in two days with a bivouac below the 90m diedre. 1100m. ED – /ED with 30 pegs'. The route description goes on to enumerate about twenty pitches of V or more. Compare this with the 1980 Piola approach, 'ED *inf*/500m' (Piola takes you only ⅔ of the way up, after which you either abseil off or go on to the top via the 1952 Classic West Face route). A topographical drawing in place of the usual written description shows twelve pitches of up to VIb and two of AO 1 p.a. (A = Artificial; 0 = Easy, no need for étriers; 1 p.a. = one point of aid). Piola has added a grade ABO (abominable!) beyond ED *sup* for his modern free climbing horrors.

Under the Vallot System the technical difficulty of any ice climbing that will be found on a route is harder to tie down. The French seem to assume that anyone going to their alps is conversant with all manner of snow and ice. A useful international comparision might be:

A Comparision of some International Ice Grades

USA	Scotland	France
AI[1]	1	F
AI[2]	2	D
AI[3]	3	D*sup*
AI[4]	4	TD
WI[5]	5	TD +
WI[6]	6	ED
WI[7]	6	ED +
Note: A = Alpine Ice W = Waterfall Ice		

New Zealand has an interesting tale. Up to 1982 they successfully resisted formal grading so that climbing in the Southern Alps was pretty much a process of discovery – though of course a fair amount of information could be elicited from those who knew the area. Nor did any guidebook exist, so that you went to those mountains armed with only a little more information than the earliest pioneers. Then the conventional tide would not be contained any longer and in 1982 The Mount Cook Guide Book (Hugh Logan) was published, and with it came grades:

'The grading of routes is a controversial exercise, especially in areas where no system has been used before. This applies particularly to the Mt. Cook region where peaks are heavily glaciated and where conditions vary greatly from day to day and season to season. A system of grading has been devised, however, begining at 1- and running through to 6+. The system is intended to be open ended, and grades 7 and 8 are presumably possible. The grading criteria were, in decreasing order of importance, technical difficulty, objective danger, length, and access. The Australian rock grading system has been applied to crux passages.

'Climbers using this Guide are urged to rely on the grade only as a rough indication. Conditions vary so much at Mt. Cook that grades can often be misleading. The "guidebook" mentality is no substitute for trusting your own judgement and knowing what you are and are not capable of. In the end it comes down to reading the mountain not the book.'

So there it is. Almost every country has a grading system; some have two or three. They will all take a little getting to know; they will all have their quirks, inconsistencies and indiosyncrasies – but they will be fun. Spend some time in getting acquainted with any system that is new to you, and even then be prepared for the odd hiccup. It is perhaps better to begin easy; you can always climb harder the next time. It is not always possible the other way around.

The Himalayas, Alaska, Peru and most of the other far-flung alps of the world are seldom graded – and certainly by no uniform system. But by the time you are climbing that far afield, grades will be of little more than academic interest, the stuff of idle chat, gentle argument.

2   Equipment

Climbers, and you'll probably have been a climber before you venture to alps, are notoriously idiosyncratic in their preferences and prejudices about gear; ask any two and the chances are that they'll disagree. At the last it is a personal thing and even very experienced climbers frequently change their minds about what exactly should be carried on a route, which axe is to be preferred, or which boots work best. None of which is greatly comforting to the beginner who, reasonably, will want to know much more.

BOOTS

If you have already done some snow or ice climbing, perhaps in winter on frozen water weeps and falls, or somewhere like Scotland, you'll own a pair of boots that will almost certainly do splendidly for at least your first alpine season too. Generically there are two protagonists: leather boots and plastic boots. The latter have won a great following in recent years, so much so that a year or two ago it looked as if plastic might supersede leather altogether. That hasn't happened, however, and there's been a bit of a swing back towards leather. There are as many opinions about which material makes the best boots as there are climbers. My views, for what they are worth, may be summarised as:

1.   *Plastic*   Slightly cheaper; often lighter, sometimes longer wearing; usually fairly comfortable immediately, but seldom ever fitting like a glove – even when ancient. Good with crampons, superb on ice and mixed routes; not so good or so friendly on pure rock. Frequently warmer than single leather boots because they are nearly always supplied with an inner – which provides both comfort and insulation.

2.   *Leather*   Slightly   dearer;   usually heavier; perhaps not so rugged. Often not very comfortable to begin but when worn-in they can be as foot-friendly as a pair of carpet slippers. Better on pure rock than most plastic boots and very nearly as good on ice and mixed. Single leather boots are not as warm as most plastic boots; double leather boots are much heavier than their plastic counterparts.

Again for what it's worth, I prefer a well worn-in leather boot for summer alpine use because I find them more comfortable, especially over those long days that end (all too often) in hot, toe-stubbing descents, and because I can rock climb better in them. For winter alpine use (which is an unlikely, but not impossible, time for your first season) plastic scores fairly heavily. A double plastic boot – and most are already double anyway – is much lighter than a double leather boot, even if you can find one of the latter these days. Moreover since most of an alpine winter day is spent with crampons on, the leather boot's greater affinity with rock is no longer a significant factor. What is more important than any of that is that whatever genus of boot you opt for and whatever breed within that genus, the fit is crucial. You may wear them for as

Fig 11   Leather and plastic mountaineering boots (left to right): Asolo AFS101s, plastic; Koflach Ultra Extreme, plastic; Asolo 8000 – leather double boots for high altitude or alpine winter use, light for a double leather boot but still heavier than the equally warm combination of plastic boots and aveolite inners (see page 187). Nevertheless the construction of the 8000 is a work of art and the most comfortable warm boot I've ever worn.

much as 18 hours a day, the greater part of which will be unadulterated misery if your boots don't fit. Try them in the shop with the thickness of socks (one or two pairs according to preference) that you'd wear on the hill. Be fussy – they're your feet and it's your pocket. Walk up and down. Beware if the boots are at all tight, for although leather boots will usually stretch a little with use, and although plastic boots can be heat-stretched in some shops, it is *much* better if they fit right in the first place. Nor are your own feet the best implements for stretching boots – though someone else's can be if you should find a volunteer! Tight boots are cold boots too, because they restrict the blood's circulation around the feet. Too large boots, on the other hand (or rather, foot) will slip and rub and blister. So take care in selection.

Any good outdoor retailer will advise you on a reasonable pair of alpine boots. Features that are worth looking for are hook and ring lacing; padded ankles, a solid composition rubber sole with a vibram, Jannu or similar pattern; a welt at toe and heel to accommodate step-in crampon bindings; a sewn-in bellows tongue to discourage snow

31

and water; and a fairly stiff sole the better to retain crampons for snow and ice work. Old hands used to say that a good pair of boots cost a week's wages. That adage seems still to hold roughly true.

Another thought on boots. There are scores of alpine routes, ridges, scrambles and easy climbs – up to AD, say – where the most efficient footwear is not a traditional mountain boot, whether of plastic or leather, with its stiff sole, high ankle and fair few pounds of weight, but a pair of a newer generation of boots which have no generic name that I can find but which are commonly available in almost all outdoor shops. Such footwear is lighter, gentler to feet and robust enough for the alpine day. Where such a boot will go and go well it seems sensible to take it: the best fit. They are not suitable for steep or technical snow and ice climbing, indeed the very expectation of such ground would disqualify them. They are good, however, for rocky scrambles and they will accept crampons – though not all crampons and certainly not those with step-in bindings. Care needs to be taken in the fitting of the crampon which is, if anything, even more critical than with standard mountain boots. Take a flexible view: it's horses for courses and there are many courses where light-weight boots will speed and gladden your day, conceding neither sure-footedness nor safety. (*see* Fig 16)

As proof of this pudding I recall a mate of mine, Rob Collister, alpiniste extra-

Fig 12   A lightweight and an orthodox plastic mountaineering boot compared.

ordinaire, who traversed the Meije, the Pave and Grande Ruine and a fair few more in a three-day jaunt in a pair of lightweight boots such as those shown in the photograph. It was he who convinced me. *Educated* he might say!

CRAMPONS

If, as I would recommend, you have already climbed on snow and ice in crampons, you will be as fixed in your prejudices on these instruments as any other climber − and you need read no further into this section. However, for those coming to snow and ice, or at least to crampons, for the first time, here is more on the subject.

Oscar Eckenstein is generally credited with having invented the 10-point crampon in 1908. Since that day the features representing progress, apart from metallurgical advances, that have left us with lighter, stronger crampons, are:

1. The addition of two forward protruding points (the lobster claws of the 12-point crampon, invented by Laurent Grivel in 1932).
2. A steady improvement in the means of fastening. I anticipate that all straps will soon be replaced by cable clip-ons, or 'step-

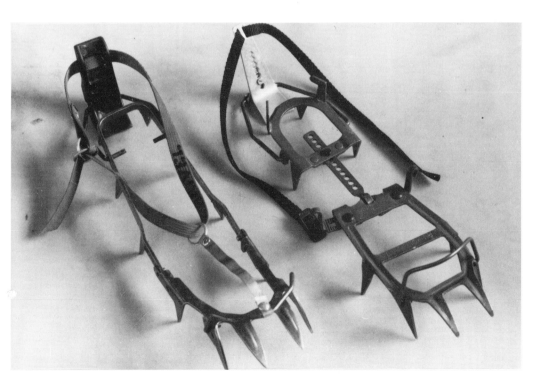

Fig 13 Two modern 12-point, step-in, adjustable crampons: left 'Grivel' F2, rigid or articulated on the same model; right, Stubai 'Tirol', articulated.

Fig 14   Two conventionally-fastened articulated adjustable crampons: left, Salewa Classic, right Salewa Everest.

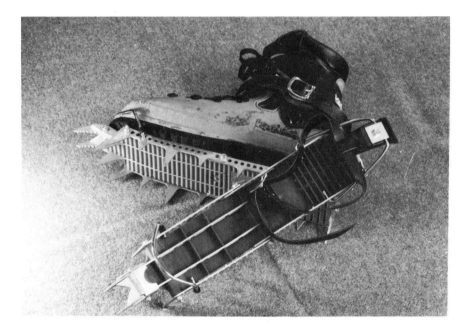

Fig 15   Lowe Footfangs.

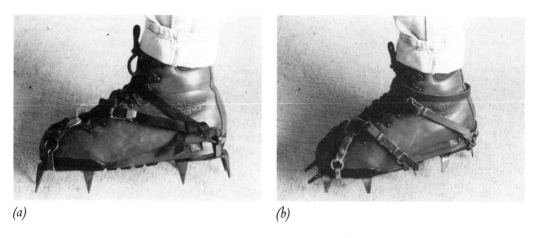

Fig 16   Lightweight boots with (a) 10-point crampons, and (b) 12-point crampons.

ins' which are not unlike some ski bindings.
3.   Greater ease of adjustment in width and length.
4.   A choice of a rigid or articulated crampon (and, in some cases, that choice on the same crampon).

Most stores will stock over half a dozen different kinds of 12-point crampon, which, with their close relatives such as Footfangs, are the only serious suitors for the ice climber's foot. If you have taken my hint on lightweight boots for alpine walks, scrambles and easy routes you'll pay a slight crampon penalty. Such footwear won't wear step-in bindings: they're out. Nor will they accept any other crampon with the same comforting, clamp-like sureness of a specialist mountain boot. This is, as I believe Americans say, the down-side. But they will take strap-on crampons and take them well enough for glacier crossings, simple snow slopes and those patches of snow or névé that you are likely to encounter during a rock or ridge scramble. Take extra care in the fitting and test the fit with a trot on some grass before leaving the campsite.

For walking, scrambling and for very

easy alpine climbs you could get by with a pair of 10-point crampons, though, other than being cheaper, 10-pointers afford no advantage over 12-pointers – indeed they concede a point or two. For the sake of a few pounds saved it hardly seems worth sacrificing those extra points. They'll come in useful before your alpine ambitions have taken you beyond very many summits. (*see* Fig 18)

As for 12-point crampons, you will be faced with an initial choice of rigid or articulated (except in the case of Grivel F2s which ingeniously offer that choice on the same crampon). Rigid crampons, Footfangs included, are designed for climbing solely on ice (Footfangs for water-ice, on which they are incomparable), but unless you intend to devote your energies exclusively to that substance – and there's more fun to be had elsewhere – I'd advise against a rigid crampon for general alpine use. In any case, modern plastic boots are themselves so stiff that they render rigidity in a crampon almost redundant. Rigid crampons, being subject to greater stresses than their flexible counterparts, break more frequently. They also ball-up more readily and do not perform

35

so well on mixed ground – that is, a mixture of rock, snow and ice – which is common in the alps. However, since there is at least one model now available that converts from rigid to articulated in seconds, it may soon be that no choice has to be made. For the moment, if choice must be made, go for a hinged or articulated model.

You may be confronted with a further choice: there are two ways of arranging the front-points. These may be called standard and French front-points, since the second arrangement occurs most commonly on crampons of French design and manufacture. In use, the difference may be summarised thus: standard front-points work well on every kind of terrain; French front-points work particularly well on névé and on ice, but rather badly on mixed ground. This is because the lower pair of points bend to deny the upper ones free access to the rock.

The decision should be a fairly simple one: if you intend to climb on all manner of terrain, which in alpine country is likely, and can afford only one pair of crampons, choose front-points of standard design. If, however, you intend to disport yourself exclusively on snow and ice, you will do well to invest in crampons with French front-points. If money is no object, you can own both and the world is your oyster. Grivel give a choice of front-points on their F2 model but it is one or the other – they are not interchangeable on the same crampon.

The most common makers of 12-point crampons are Salewa, Grivel, Chouinard, SMC, Inter Alp, Laprade, Cassin, Stubai, and Charlet-Moser. Footfangs, made by Lowe, work on all terrain, like other crampons, but were designed specifically for steep water-ice on which surface they perform best, and where they arguably outperform traditional 12-pointers. Some Footfang fans claim that they are least as good as any other crampon on any other terrain. I am not convinced.

Fig 17 To front-point or not to front-point: curves and angles. Those marked A are standard front-point arrangements, some curved some angled; B sports 'French' front-points, while C, being a 10-point crampon, has no front-points at all.

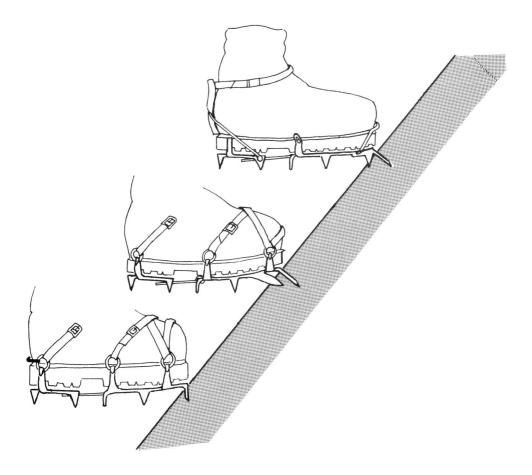

Fig 18 ~Top: standard front-points; centre: French; bottom: 10-pointers.

Fit and Fastening

Major considerations in the selection of crampons are weight (the lighter the better), fit, and security of fastening. Fit and security are crucial and worth a careful look. If your crampons come off, the chances are that you will too. With good boots, however, and with correctly fitted, properly attached crampons, that is an easily avoided embarrassment.

Conventional teaching says that crampons ought to spring-fit the boots – that they should stay on a shaken boot without straps. I would argue that a fraction less than a spring-fit is the ideal. If your crampon fits your boot snugly when tinkering at home, the chances are that it will be too snug, infuriatingly snug, in some wild and sprindrift-swept gully, which is the sort of place you'll end up putting them on. So, good fit, but a slack

37

Fig 19   A good fit: Asolo AFS101's and Grivel F2 Crampons mate well.

spring, perhaps. Some kinds of crampon have a wire heel-bar. If this is the case, ensure that the bar fits along the welt at the heel of the boot. Whilst a heel-bar is not essential, such an arrangement does afford greater security.

Some models of plastic boot have deep heels and you may need to replace the heel-bar with a longer piece of wire in order to locate it in the heel welt. This can be done easily at home with nothing more than a pair of pliers. It may take an hour of juggling with adjustments in length and width before you achieve a satisfactory fit, but once completed they should need no further alteration, unless, as sometimes happens, that good fit deteriorates into something sloppier at their first battering.

In that case, a second look that night, with some minor tampering, and those crampons should fit your boots for ever, though new boots are likely to mean new adjustments. When correctly fitted, the front-points should project beyond the toe of the boot by ¾ – 1in (2 – 3cm). A piece of thin card placed at the toe of the boot will show more clearly by how much the front-points project.

Fastening crampon to boot is completed by means of straps or, more recently, cable bindings and step-in bindings. All sorts of patent straps are available. Go for the simplest – four neoprene straps (two per boot) with hole and pin buckles are as good as any. Whatever your choice, the straps should be of waterproof material or coated

Fig 20   Gauging the front-point projection.

in some way to prevent the accumulation of snow and ice. Crampons are often purchased free of straps, in which case you will have to fit them yourself. This is a simple process. Follow the manufacturer's instructions carefully and remember that all buckles should lie on the outside of the boot so that one set of buckles cannot snag on the other, perhaps tripping an otherwise flawless performance.

The method of passing the straps through the forward rings merits attention. The straps are locked by passing them through from the outside on both posts. This system also prevents the section of the strap that passes over the toes from sliding forward off the toe – and possibly off the boot (*see* Fig 22). A faster but equally secure system, which avoids the threading of the front rings, is to join the two front rings with a separate strap, or two shorter straps joined by a ring, through which the remaining

Fig 21   Neoprene straps with hole-and-pin buckles. Note the two turns on the heel strap.

Fig 22   Detail of arrangement of straps at the toe.

Fig 23   Scotch rings.

foot strap is passed (*see* Fig 23). The Scots call this variation French rings and the Americans call them Scot rings! By whatever name, the length of the joined front straps is critical. If the loop formed by connecting the straps with a ring is too long it will be pulled, when tightened from the ankle, far along your boot towards the ankle. There, it can no longer do its job of holding the front of the crampon to the toe of the boot. On the other hand, if the same loop is too small, you may not be able to pull it over the toe of the boot in the first place, in which case it is useless. So arrange your rings with care, and don't take it for granted that, fitting one pair of boots perfectly, they will necessarily fit a second pair. Some makes of boots are bulkier than others, even when they advertise the same foot size.

Crampon straps may be secured to the crampons by tying, threading or riveting; all seem to be equally satisfactory. Straps should be tight enough to hold boot and crampon together on the roughest ground, but not so tight that they restrict the foot's circulation. This is a problem with leather boots, but less of one with plastic, thanks to its rigid shell. Some ankle straps go around the ankle once, others twice. The latter give greater security but whichever you choose, the strap should be long enough after the buckle is fastened to be gripped easily with a gloved hand.

In recent years cable and step-in bindings have improved enormously. When properly fitted – and fitting here is crucial – they are superb, though a sceptical and conservative climbing population may take some time to be won over. Their advantages are:

1.   No straps to break or to restrict circulation, so feet are warmer and safer.
2.   Speed – no fiddling with straps, rings and buckles with frozen fingers. This is an essential advantage on one of those routes that have you donning and doffing crampons every other pitch.

Their disadvantages are that they must be adjusted to fit perfectly. They tend to fit imperfectly on leather boots because such boots usually lack pronounced welts at heel and toe which are essential for a secure cable or step-in fitting. On the other hand, most plastic boots have a veritable ledge of a welt at heel and toe, tailor-made for step-in bindings. The two most popular (and the best) step-in bindings of the 1985–86 season were to be found on the Salewa Messner crampon and the Grivel F2. Competition should increase the choice and decrease the price. I spent a winter in leather boots trying to kick off a pair of crampons fastened with step-in bindings, without success. Properly fitted they work well, especially on plastic boots.

Care and Maintenance

After use, check crampons to see that screws have not worked loose, that straps or bindings are in good fettle, and that rivets are still holding good. Have a look, too, at the metal of the crampon, checking for cracks or other signs of metal fatigue – particularly after heavy use. Check for sharpness, and re-sharpen only as frequently as necessary, which may be often if you alternate climbing on mixed ground with climbing on ice. Water-ice demands sharp front-points; snow-ice can be subdued with blunter instruments. Sharpen by hand with a file, never with a powered grindstone as the heat may degrade the temper. Sharpen the down-points to a point and the front-points from the top to a chisel edge.

Choose your crampons carefully. Fit them with even greater care and attach them securely. They turn smooth and potentially dangerous snow and ice slopes into the gentlest and friendliest of places.

ICE-AXES

As with crampons, if you already know the snow and ice climbing game, you will know too what you need and like. Beyond that, the axe or axes you carry will largely be dictated by the nature of the route you are to climb. An easy snow climb at a gentle angel will demand only an unspectacular axe; as will an alpine rock route with an easy but snow-bound approach and descent. (On some rock routes you may be able to dispense with an axe altogether – though

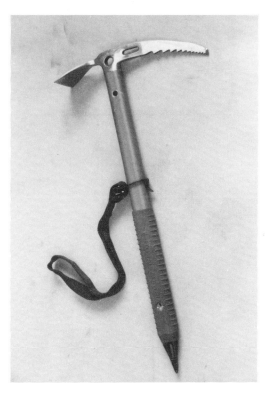

Fig 25   A standard alpine axe. This model has a shaft of adjustable length so that it can be converted from a 'walking' to a 'climbing' axe.

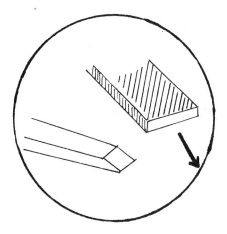

Fig 24   Sharpen to a chisel point

these will be exceptions.) A technical north face, however, will bring the best out of any two of the best tools on the market, whilst a steep purely ice route is clearly best addressed in full ice regalia. As with most alpine things you match your gear to the route and try to take only what you anticipate will be necessary; and therein lies the essence of it – what will be necessary.

In my book *Snow and Ice Climbing* I had much more to say on the subject of axes and I think it may be prudent to say some of it again to those who have wandered straight from summer crag to alp. (Those who came by the longer way via snow and ice climbing need read here no longer.)

The axe is the most important tool in the Alpine trade and there is a bewildering array to choose from. Fortunately most of the axes on the retailer's shelf work well enough under most circumstances. Proof of that, if proof is needed, is supplied by any cluster of mountaineers. Ask any ten which axe they prefer and you'll probably get ten different answers. Take some comfort from the discord – it means that almost any modern axe will do for almost everything, but some additional information will help you make the choice.

It used to be simpler, and not so many years ago – twenty, at most. At that time all axes had wooden shafts, usually very long ones, and they all had picks emerging, more or less at right angles, from the shaft. On gentle slopes they were little more than walking sticks; on steeper slopes they cut holds for hand or foot. These uses dictated the length and shape of the axe. Then – and it is difficult to say precisely when or where – a revolution occurred. Of this revolution Chouinard says in *Climbing Ice*:

'On a rainy summer day in 1966, I went on to a glacier in the Alps with the purpose of testing every different type of ice-axe available at the time. My plan was to see which one worked best for *piolet ancre*, which one was better at step-cutting, and why. After I found a few answers, it took the intervention of Donald Snell to convince the very reluctant and conservative Charlet factory to make a 55cm axe with a curved pick for the crazy American. In those days a 55cm axe was crazy enough – but a curved pick! I had the feeling that modifying the standard straight pick into a curve compatible with the arc of the axe's swing would allow the pick to stay put better in the ice. I had noticed that a standard pick would often pop out when I place my weight on it. My idea worked'.

A few years later Rob Collister wrote in *Mountain*:

'The development of a curved pick for axes and hammers was an event in ice climbing history comparable with the introduction of crampons in the 1890s, or the use of front-points and ice pitons in the 1930s. It could prove more revolutionary than either. Since it makes for both greater speed and security, it will encourage those who have previously been deterred by the need to choose between the two'.

Doubtless the French, Germans and Austrians have their version of this revolution too, but sometime in the later 1960s axes changed shape. Axe picks were drooped. Chouinard achieved this by *curving* the picks steeply downwards; MacInnes (on his prototype Terrordactyls) by *angling* his picks steeply downwards, at an angle of about 55 degrees between pick and shaft. Using these new tools a climber could hang his entire weight on an axe and it wouldn't pop out – even on vertical ice. This meant that instead of climbing ice by hours of laborious step-cutting, a climber with a new axe in either hand could attack the steepest ice front on, the most natural way.

Chouinard claims, and he may well be right, that this technique was first used in California in 1967. The French christened it *piolet traction*. The English-speaking world call it front-pointing. The effect was dramatic. Times for routes were halved, then decimated. Even the hardest alpine ice routes were soloed – such was the efficiency and security afforded by these new tools – and step-cutting died a short death, despite attempts by traditionalists to drag it out for an indecently long time. I have never cut an ice step in my life except in demonstration, though the odd one can still be used to good effect. The ice-axe and its relatives such as the ice-hammer merit closer inspection.

The Shaft

The traditional shaft was made of ash or hickory. Its day has passed. Laminated bamboo enjoyed a short vogue, particularly on Chouinard axes. Few modern axes are wooden-shafted, although there are able climbers who still prefer the feel of a good, straight-grained hickory shaft. Fibreglass has been used for making shafts, though they have never proved to be really popular. Perhaps the feel is not right or folk are wary of the variation in strength to which this material is prone at low temperatures. A coating of fibreglass can also be used to strengthen any wooden-shafted axe, but at the cost of greater weight. The most

common materials for today's axe shafts are metal – aluminium and titanium being recent contenders – and carbonfibre, which is more recent still. A bare metal shaft is cold to hold, and cold hands must be avoided. Coating a metal shaft in a moulded rubber or neoprene grip largely solves this problem, as well as giving the axe a better feel and dampening most of the vibration consequent upon a hefty blow to hard ice.

The ideal length for an ice-axe shaft is one of those subjects of perennial – and often heated – debate amongst climbers. No two people seem to agree, and when they do, one will quickly change his mind. As a rough guide only, 70cm is generally held to be the order of length for an alpine axe for glacier travel and easier alpine routes that do not inovlve technical ice-climbing – the spike just scrapes the ground when the axe is held by the head. Then, again roughly, the steeper the climb, or the more confined its nature, the shorter the axe. The shortest anyone would want to go is 36cm (the length of a Terrordactyl's shaft), and many prefer something comparatively long, perhaps 55–65cm even on vertical ice. It is a matter of individual preference and some experience – not much more. If it helps, I have climbed on everything from Scottish gullies, to Welsh water-ice, to alpine north faces, to the Himalayas with the same two axes for the last ten years. They both have 40cm shafts and although I have flirted with others, I always return to them. Some use two short axes for steep technical ground, but a longer 70cm axe for easier alpine work. The permutations are endless – as are the arguments. Use a 70cm axe on easier alpine terrain and start on steep ice with two 40–50cm tools and you won't go far wrong. A shaft with a flattened oval cross-section is the most comfortable shape to

*Fig 26   Axe heads: picks and adzes.
Shown here is an axe with adze and pick of
standard alpine inclination and one of more
extreme – specialist – inclination.*

hold, while a ribbed, rubber moulding gives
a better grip.

The Head (Pick and Adze)

Most of today's heads are made from high-
quality steel. It matters little whether they
are chrome molybdenum or titanium, they
all work well. Balance and weight are
important, however. It is not uncommon to
see a climbing shop filled with climbers
carefully fondling axes as a gun-fighter
might his guns, or scything the air in an
imaginary move on some imaginary climb as
a gladiator might practise a swipe with his
chosen weapon. Once again, only experience will enable you to make an educated
selection. Ask friends; solicit opinions of
those more experienced; borrow before you
buy.

A problem with opinions is that they
vary. While some prefer heavy-headed axes,
arguing that they make for a penetrating
blow, others choose light heads, arguing
that every ounce saved is energy conserved.
There's no absolute answer. My axe has
weights that I can attach to the head by
means of an allen screw, so I am able to
make it lighter or heavier as the whim takes
me. In fact, I've climbed with all four
weights on, and all four off, and have found
the difference negligible.

Pick Profiles

There are three basic pick profiles – curved,
inclined or angled, and banana, which is
really an inclined pick with a bit of French
flair added – to some good effect. There is
not much to choose between them. I prefer
inclined or banana picks but wouldn't lose
any sleep if invited to climb with a curve. I
have never conducted a survey, but I suspect
that curves are more popular than angles on
moderate alpine ground, while angles (or
banana's) are the preferred shape on steeper
stuff. I am told that there is now an
'elephant' pick. This is S-shaped. Its
relationship to jumbo is not obvious unless
it is in the trunk. I am told that such picks
work well, although not discernibly better
than bananas. The ingenuity of man and the
fecundity of his terminology suggest that
there is plenty of scope for more exotic
breeding. At the moment it looks as if
ornithologists rule the nominal roost –
vultures, eagles, Terrordactyls – with

Fig 27　Pick profiles (top to bottom): curve (in this case gently); banana; and angle.

teeth stop the axe from wobbling in the ice; they are not there to prevent the pick from slipping out, as the angle of the pick alone does that. Many manufacturers, Simond on his Chacal and Barracuda tools included, cut their teeth too long. After some experimentation you may find that you want to file down some of the more aggressive fangs. I reduced those on my own axe to less than half the original length before I could extract it with anything less than a monumental effort. A good axe should go in easily, stay in, and come out when asked. An axe which takes more effort to extract than insert needs to be doctored, or detuned. But go slowly; it is more difficult to re-cut the teeth than it is to remove them. A favourite axe of mine had but three tiny milk teeth. The angle of its pick was steep and it held in ice without worry, allowing itself to be withdrawn without persuasion. Since then, the manufacturers, bowing to fashion rather than efficiency, have serrated the thing along its entire under-length. It looks like Jaws and works no better than the original.

The banana pick (*see* Fig 27) is really a modification of the inclined pick and is designed to make extraction easier, although not everyone agrees that it achieves this. In my opinion banana picks work well, although since that opinion is based on experience all too often gained *in extremis*, it is difficult to be sure whether its efficiency is the result of a good design or a good day. Certainly a trembling 100ft run out is no laboratory test.

zoologists, vegetarians and fishmongers filling the minor placings with chacals, bananas and barracudas.

For straightforward alpine routes up to AD, a general purpose 70cm shafted axe with a gently curving pick and an adze shaped to cut the odd step is fine.

Most axes for serious climbing are equipped with picks, whatever their profile, at about 55–65 degrees to the shaft, and they all work. Picks should be thin (for penetration) but strong – no easy combination. A set of teeth – no more than four or five are really needed – should feature on the underside at the tip. These

Adzes

Adzes are designed primarily for one of two jobs. Large, shovel-like, steeply inclined adzes, such as those found on the

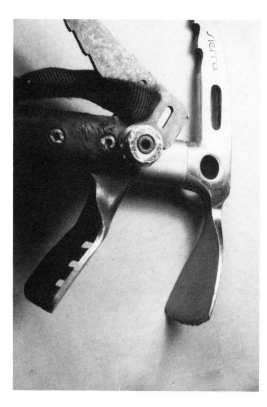

Fig 28   Adzes: top, a conventional alpine adze; bottom, the inclined shovel-like adze of the Simond Barracuda, an excellent steep ice tool.

chopping stances at belays and clearing away soft or rotten snow and ice in order to reveal the good stuff in which to place ice-screws.

Specialised Picks and Adzes

Jeff Lowe, the celebrated and innovative American ice climber has developed an axe with a pick which is a hollow tube. He christened it the Hummingbird. It was designed with steep water-ice in mind and that is where it works best – the hollow tube displacing less ice than a conventional pick which makes it both easier to place and less likely to shatter cold, brittle ice. Unless you intend to climb exclusively on frozen waterfalls, however, such a weapon is almost certainly more specialised than you need.

More and more manufacturers are furnishing axes (and hammers) with inter-changeable picks. Clearly these are the most versatile of the lot, but be sure to fasten your selected pick well. A loose pick is disconcerting; a lost one disastrous.

Spikes

Spikes are pretty much spikes. They should be kept reasonably sharp for penetrating snow up to névé consistency, but not weapon-sharp, when they can be dangerous, to mates as well as to the owner.

Ice Hammers

Modern ice hammers are essentially axes with a hammer-head in the place of the adze. Most climbers on technical alpine ice carry one of each: an adze in case steps have to be cut or in case loose snow is encountered; a hammer for driving pitons, snargs,

Terrordactyl and Barracuda axes, are made for climbing steep, less-than-solid snow, where the rule is the more steeply inclined the adze (up to 60 degrees) and the bigger, the better. Such adzes will cut ice and snow for steps but not as well as the more conventional adze which was made for that job. Conventional adzes are correspondingly less efficient when climbing less than solid snow. My choice would be a Terrordactyl/Barracuda-type adze which will do very well for the few steps you are likely to cut. Secondary tasks, which both types of adze perform satisfactorily, include

Fig 29   Two hammer heads. The top hammer, a Stubai, has interchangeable picks.

picks will benefit from a certain amount of de-tuning. Avoid the use of power tools for they will degrade the temper of the metal. Tradition has it that old-timers carry a file on their person so that some sharpening of crampons and axe can be conducted *en route*. I have yet to spot this in practice, but it is not a bad habit.

Tools that have adjustable or interchangeable components should be checked daily to see that screws and bolts are all snug.

Slings and Wrist Loops

For easy alpine routes – say, up to and including AD – a general purpose axe such as the one shown on page 41 will do very well. But for steeper climbing your axes and hammers will need to be equipped with a sling and wrist loop. You may buy your tool with the maker's sling already in place. These are generally more than adequate. They are easy to replace with a new one when worn or, if you prefer, a home-made version. Half or one-inch (15 or 25mm) climbing tape is ideal for this purpose and if you are adept at DIY, you can engineer a loop with a local broadening around the wrist in order to reduce pressure and increase comfort. Hands will be warmer too because their blood supply will be less restricted – a blood supply that has a hard time flowing uphill all day as it is.

Whether patent or home-made, the sling should be of such a length that when you hold it in your preferred manner, your fist encircles the shaft very close to its end. Try climbing when holding the shaft about half-way up and you'll quickly appreciate how much more efficient it is to hold it at the end. Some like to rest by crooking their elbow into the wrist loop, in which case the

etc. Axes and hammers may or may not be the same length; again it's a matter of preference. Some climbers carry three tools (useful on long climbs if one tool breaks), in which case the combination is likely to be two axes and one hammer. Two adzes are twice as good as one in unconsolidated or melting snow, and it is possible, if not entirely satisfactory, to drive pitons and snargs and to start ice-screws with an axe if your hammer breaks. Only a pessimist, and a rich one at that, would carry two of each.

Maintenance

Keep your ice tools rust-free and sharpen them as often as necessary with a hard file. Stick to the original shape, although, as previously mentioned, some long-toothed loop has to be big enough to take the owner's forearm, encased, as it is likely to be, in several layers of sleeve.

Point of Attachment

A wrist loop is usually attached to the axe at one of two points; at the head or at some point along the shaft (though always above the hand). All axes will have a hole or slot through which the wrist loop may be knotted (always using a tape knot) and here lies the root of another argument: where to attach.

Those who prefer to attach to a hole provided at some point in the shaft claim that this ensures that the wrist loop, when weighted, will follow the line of the shaft more faithfully, and that this, in turn, encourages the pick into the ice, rather than out of it. The argument is a reasonable one. My only objection to a mid-shaft attachment is a difficulty that arises on mixed ground when axes that have been dropped to your wrists, while your hands seize holds, are likely to dangle horizontally and catch in the mountainside. I have such an axe, a Barracuda, and have chosen to ignore the maker's preferred attachment hole about two-thirds of the way up the shaft because on mixed ground it caught with infuriating efficiency. I have attached the wrist loop to the head, where there is a slot, though whether it is provided for that purpose I do not know. No matter, the axe is now a model of convenience, dangles harmlessly vertical from the wrist, and the 3in (7.5cm) between the two possible points of attachment make no difference to its technical virtuosity that I can discern.

If, by attaching your wrist loop to the head of your axe (or hammer) you are worried that the resultant pull may not be in the same axis as the shaft – that is, straight downwards – then you can tape the wrist loop (with sticky tape) or tie it (with line or climbing tape in a small loop) to the shaft, a few inches above the hand.

Other methods of achieving this involve winding the wrist loop around the shaft. I do not recommend these because, whilst the winding is an easy enough operation standing on the ground at the beginning of a climb, it is a considerable evolution *in extremis*, after you have let go of your axes in order to use your hands, for whatever reason. Using more convenional 'straight' wrist loops, axes that have been dropped to the wrist can be brought to hand simply with a flick of that wrist.

SLINGS AND AXES

Axe slings should be carefully checked for wear and tear. There will be times when your entire weight (and therefore life) hangs on them and a shredded sling is an unneccessary excitement. Opinions vary on the desirability of using an axe sling on less steep or walking terrain. The disadvantages are:

1. The axe follows you closely if you fall and may clout body and head during the descent, although you shouldn't be falling on this sort of ground.
2. It is awkward to change from hand to hand when zigzagging up snow slopes (when the axe is best carried on the inside hand).

The advantages are:

1. It is conveniently to hand.
2. It is difficult to drop.

3. It affords some support when cutting steps.

It is possible to achieve the best of both worlds by having an ice-axe sling with a loop in the end so that it may be threaded and unthreaded. Then on easy ground you can, if you wish, carry your axe without a sling, attaching only on steeper terrain. Another solution is to leave the sling on the axe but to let it hang free, not taking it to hand, where you are happy to do that.

On steep ground the sling and wrist loops are such an essential part of the axe and of the climbing technique employed that dissent is plain daft. Another argument rages over whether axes held in hand by sling and wrist loop should be further secured to the body by a sling or line, long enough not to restrict an arms-length reach. Here the disadvantages are:

1. The axe follows closely if you fall and may punish you severely for your error or bad luck.
2. The sling tangles easily (some would say incessantly, and still others would add, inextricably) with body and equipment.

The advantages are:

1. Once your fall has been arrested you know where to find your axe (you may even be impaled on it).
2. It can be cast aside with impunity to deal with a rock handhold, or to attend to equipment or bodily functions, and can be readily retrieved.
3. If the long sling or line is strong enough and of the right length it can be used to hang in for a rest. I have seen ice climbers who have contrived a sling which joins them to their axe and which can be adjusted by

means of a single pull through a simple buckle so that it can be snugged-up in order to hang by it for a breather. Since I have never been able to contemplate so complicated a manoeuvre it would be equally unfair were I to commend or condemn. It seems sensible to master the simple things first, then by all means give it a go if you wish.
4. The axe can still be swapped from hand to hand.

Stowing the Axe

If axe or hammer need to be stowed for some period this is best done by means of a holster attached to the harness, although old-timers insist that it must be pushed

Fig 30   Axes in holsters on harnesses.

Fig 31 *Axe in holster threaded to a rucksack's hip-belt.*

Fig 32 *An axe stowed in compression straps.*

(a)

(b)

Fig 33 *Stowing an axe between shoulder and sack.*

down between sack and back from over one shoulder. Whether holster or shoulder-borne, care should be taken not to drop the implement. If you anticipate that you are stowing your axe for some time, slide it into the compression straps found on the side of most modern rucksacks, rather than attaching it to the ice-axe loops at the rear, where, once attached, it will be uselessly inaccessible (*see* Fig 32).

RUCKSACKS

Every alpinist needs a rucksack. A smallish one, say 30 – 40 litres will be big enough for early, single day needs. Later, on more ambitious climbs you may need a bigger sack but it's worth waiting a season or two before you invest in one. Fortunately there are dozens of very good models available – the consumer having benefited from intense competition between rival manufacturers. To make their carriage more comfortable alpine sacks are stiffened with internal frames or by padding or, best of all, by a combination of both. Some models have adjustable harness systems while others come in differing back lengths. Choose with care, get the back size right in the shop and buy a sack that is big enough for your needs but no bigger (or more expensive) than those needs. The basic requirements of any alpine sack include resistance to wear and tear and to water, though few are completely waterproof (whatever the manufacturers claim). A simple poly bag will quickly and cheaply waterproof any sack should you consider that necessary – which for the alps is questionable.

A sack should fit comfortably at the hips (a padded hip belt is a very good thing) and lie comfortably between hips and

shoulders – and close to the back so that the load is *with* you rather than *behind* you. External box-pockets on the sides are a matter of personal taste, but generally an alpine sack is as well without them. Perhaps detachable pockets give you the best of both worlds; a capacious valley sack and a sleeker

Fig 34   A Karrimor Alpiniste contentedly packed. This is a 65-litre model, bigger than is needed for single day routes. The crampons on the top of the sack can be rendered more sociable by disarming the points with rubber protectors. Indeed in some countries – Switzerland, for example – the law obliges such protection (and for the adzes, picks and spikes of axes too) when these implements are carried on the outside of a sack.

51

Fig 35   A sack should have a comfortable and close fit.

alpine version. A wide pack can be cumbersome in a tight place such as a chimney.

Other essential features are zip pocket in the top flap for easy access to frequently needed items such as glacier cream, lipsalve, snacks, camera, water bottle, guidebook and map; a strong loop securely stitched into the top of the back so that a rope may be attached and the sack hauled when a pitch is too hard to be climbed with it on your back; at least two loops and straps by which to attach ice tools; and some system for attaching crampons to the outside of the sack from where they can be readily removed for use during a climb. (If your crampons are likely to remain on the sack for some time, as on the way up or down from a hut, for example, it may be better to stow them inside the sack's main compartment.) Some sacks have an extendable, sewn-in

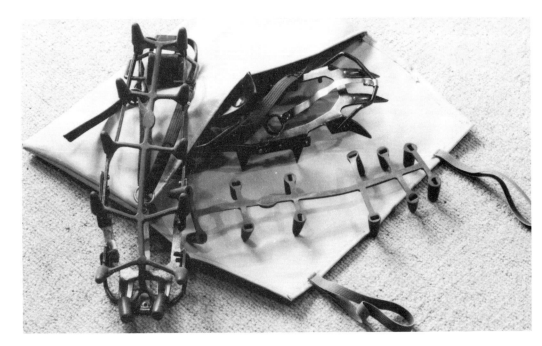

Fig 36   Crampon protectors, and the bag which Grivel supply with their F2s.

52

Fig 37   Carrying crampons inside the sack: they are less of a danger to fellow contents if disarmed in the helmet.

bivouac sleeve and though this can be useful it is not as satisfactory in a bivouac as full-scale bivi bag (*see* page 59). Bright-coloured sacks are more easily seen and there are times when there's advantage in that, apart from which, they're more cheerful.

A well packed sack can be a joy to carry, a badly packed one a pain. Sacks for the first season's routes really shouldn't be all that heavy (*see* page 65 for suggested contents), though carelessly packed items can render even the lightest sack uncomfortable.

HELMETS

There are very few alpine routes on which a helmet may safely be left behind; generally speaking they're '*de rigueur*'. Very easy angled snow routes that are, for their entire length, unexposed to the danger of falling rock or falling ice or avalanche, and with no possibility of a slip, might be such routes.

(a)   *(b)*   *(c)*

Fig 38   (a) to (c): Three ways of carrying the rope.

53

But *they* are few, and miles between. It's a good habit to get into, wearing a helmet. Get as light and comfortable a one as carries the UIAA stamp of approval.

Alpine helmets are made by Snowdon Mouldings and Phoenix (Great Britain); Galibier and Petzl (France); Salewa and Edelrid (Germany) and MSR of Seattle (USA), amongst others. A helmet should fit fairly snugly so that, in the event of a bash – from falling rock or a tumble – it isn't displaced. Its job is to protect the head and that's where it should stay. Most alpine helmets have adjustable cradles to make a good fit possible. Get one big enough to accommodate a thin balaclava when a cold chin says that it's necessary.

HARNESS

The simplest, easiest and most common way in which to attach a climbing rope to a climber is by means of a climbing harness. There are two broad categories: the body harness and the sit harness

For alpinism, continental Europeans tend to favour the body harness, claiming that it is safer and more comfortable to fall into and on to (into crevasses, for example) and that, once fallen, the victim will hang from the point of attachment at the chest in an upright position. These are generally reasonable claims. A big disadvantage, however, is that the business of donning and doffing clothing to regulate temperature is a

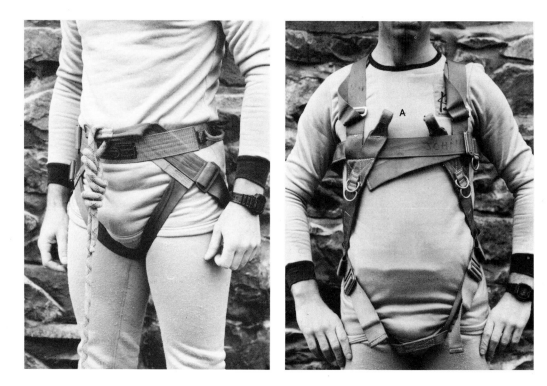

Fig 39   Harnesses: left, a DMM alpine sit-harness; right, a full body harness. The point of attachment is shown at A.

great inconvenience when trussed in the shoulder straps of both sack and harness. And, of course, they weigh far more too.

Sit harnesses are favoured by most of the rest of the world; particularly in the USA, Canada, Britain and New Zealand. The theory that, with the point of attachment sited below the body's centre of gravity, a fall will result in the victim hanging supinely horizontal from the waist, seems not to be borne out in practice. And if there is a tendency for a free hanging victim of a fall to incline backwards then that inconvenience, and it is no more than that to conscious fallen at least, is more than out-weighed by the sit harness's advantages of simplicity, lightness and freedom. For 99 per cent of all alpine use sit harnesses are preferred. Moreover, during all those hours when you are moving together, both on glacier and on mountain, you will have effectively converted your sit harness to body harness by the taking of coils around your torso. You will note when practising such things as crevasse rescue that when accoutred in this way the point of attach-ment, of yourself to the rope, is raised to about chest level and that your weight is taken on back and shoulders as well as the buttocks and hips – which renders the body harness largely redundant.

There is a wide and literally dazzling array of sit harnesses available and almost all of them do the job adequately. Some firms such as DMM and Wildcountry produce sit harnesses designed specifically for alpine use and these tend to be lighter and simpler than the same firms' luxuriously upholstered specialist rock-climbing models. In truth there is not much to choose between any of them but some points to look for might be:

1. Lightness.
2. Simplicity – especially of attachment, with gear loops and other means of attaching holsters etc.
3. Adjustable leg loops – allowing the same harness to be used in a wide range of weather and climates.
4. Loo compatible – by which I mean the facility by which the leg loops may be released in order to drop trousers when the need arises – and it sometimes arises faster than the fastest undoing of a figure of eight knot – whilst, at the same time allowing the climber (or victim) to remain attached at the waist to rope and belay. Whilst this is hardly an essential feature, it is one of con-venience and in precarious alpine loos it is productive of a more relaxed performance.

ROPE

Rope for climbing in the alps is the same stuff as you have used on rock, or ice elsewhere – that is a kernmantel laid patern. You have perhaps a greater choice of diameter.

Diameter	Length	Single/ Double	Routes/Terrain
9mm	30 – 45m	Single	Alpine valley glacier travel: very easy snow routes up to PD or straight for-ward snow routes up to AD/D.
9mm	45 – 50m	Double	The most common alpine combination: good for routes of all kinds up to the highest grades.

Note: Ropes are marked (½) or (1) at both ends. The first signifies that it is a half rope

55

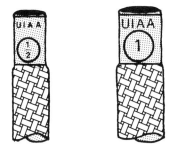

Fig 40   UIAA rope markings.

and should be used with another; the second that it is a single rope and may be used alone.

Recently a number of ropes have become available at 8.7–8.8mm. Generally these may be regarded as 9mm so that they could be used singly or doubled in the same situations; or in a combination with a 9mm. Their advantage is lightness – with very little performance sacrificed.

Many experienced alpinists climb on a combination of 9 and 7mm ropes using them together in ascent as if they were a single rope: that is clipping both through all runners – a fairly strong 16mm equivalent combination and much lighter than two 9mm ropes whilst still affording 40–45m abseil in descent.

A word more on ropes: treat your alpine rope with every bit as much care as you would back home. It is rather more prone to damage from falling rock, flailing crampons, wild axe swings, movement together on rough mixed ground and UV light – which damages perlon-based ropes and which is about in abundance at alpine altitudes. Ropes of diameters of less than

9mm are especially vulnerable to any of these abuses, the same abuse inflicting proportionally greater damage and weakening the rope proportionately more seriously.

Coiling Ropes

A badly coiled rope encourages it to twist and kink – and, as you'll already know, some ropes don't need much encouraging. On your friendly local crag a kinking is an inconvenience; on a serious alpine route it can result in hair torn out, broken marriages, dislocated partnerships, benightments and routes lost. Coil a rope carefully.

When not in use, as between seasons for example, another way to keep a rope free of kinks is to stow it loosely and randomly in a bag, feeding it from one end. A rope stowed in this way will always unravel when pulled from the upper end – try it if you're not convinced.

It is a good thing to mark your ropes at the half-way point with a felt tip pen or similar. This will conserve minutes and patience every time you need the middle of the rope.

MORE GEAR

There are a number of other items, which somehow do not seem to merit the description equipment, but which are, nevertheless, essential. Some of these are:

Goggles/Sunglasses

At alpine altitudes and reflecting off alpine snow ultraviolet light will play havoc with the eyes, causing mild conjunctivitis very quickly and snow blindness not much later.

The first is irritating, the second, with associated photophobia, painful. Sunglasses, preferably with side-pieces, are essential on all snow-covered ground, even and surprisingly perhaps, on cloudy days. A spare pair, (maybe cheapos) per party is a wise precaution in case the first is lost or damaged.

Headtorch

Since most alpine days begin in darkness (and more than a few end so) a headtorch is a vital bit of kit. They can be clipped to helmet or strapped to helmetless head, leaving both hands free to scramble, balance or climb. A spare bulb is prudent, as is a newish battery – or at least one that you are confident will last the course. If in doubt carry a spare battery too. Some headtorches are designed to be lit by lithium batteries which have the advantages of duration – up to 20 hours – and resistance to cold; they'll work at -40° which is colder than you'll want to climb. Get the lightest torch that will light the way.

Glacier Cream/Lipsalve

The alpine sun is fierce and its effect, increased by altitude and reflection, will savagely burn all but those with the darkest skins. Fair-skinned Anglo-Saxons, especially the red-headed, are particularly prone. Any exposed skin is vulnerable, not just the face. It may seem a footling thing,

Fig 41   Headtorches.

but sunburn can be painful. I know a first rate alpinist who couldn't walk in his boots for a week having sunburnt his ankles whilst lying around a base camp in a pair of tracksuit trousers that were a few inches short of his feet. But it is the face that is usually the most exposed – the ears, the nose, and the lips – which are best protected with a lipsalve or an agent thicker than that applied to the remainder of the face. The nostrils too are vulnerable to UV reflected from beneath. They are often forgotten and they are especially delicate. In any event use a sun cream such as Uvistat or Piz Buin and one with a fairly high factor of protection at least until you are well tanned. Top up your protection from time to time throughout the day. To fail on a mountain is no disgrace but to fail through sunburn is as painful as it is daft, and daft as it is avoidable.

Altimeter

A good temperature corrected aneroid barometer is a useful (though by no means essential) tool – provided the user knows how to use it and understands its implications. On a long route it will give your altitude and hence your position on that route. When navigating in misty or whiteout conditions the same information could prove vital. An altimeter, used as a barometer, will also help you anticipate changes in weather (*see* page 90). Digital altimeters are now available that will give your height to the nearest metre. They're expensive, but if it's nearly Christmas and you have a rich aunt...

Clothing

The browns, greys and khakis of the traditionalists seem at last to have been wholly swept away by the riotous splash of colour of the 'new alpinists'. Mountaineers, once the drabbest, are now the brightest people in the land. But whether a traditionalist or a brightest-is-best, most would agree that modern clothing for mountaineering is better designed and better performing than ever before.

In essence, clothing for alpinism is not greatly different from that you'll have used as a hillwalker or for climbing snow and ice in Scotland or your local equivalent. The three classic layers apply: underwear, insulating layer, shell. Underwear could be polypropylene or wool or silk, depending on preference and budget – and prejudice – but a set of longjohns and a long-sleeved vest will almost certainly feature in any alpinist's wardrobe or at least on the body or in the sack. On top of that might be breeches of wool, fibrepile or nylon (or even a nylon tracksuit) and for the torso shirts and pullovers again of wool or fibrepile.

However, once the sun is up on an alpine summer things can get decidedly hot with all that reflection. Light-coloured clothes are then far cooler and more comfortable than dark ones. Midday heat on a glacier can be surprisingly debilitating so make sure you can shed your heavy, dark clothing to reveal a light-coloured underlayer if you don't want to fry. A shell layer is a must too, either worn or carried, and might consist of Gore-tex (or similar) jacket and trousers or alternatively short jacket and salopettes or bibs of any one of the microporous materials. Shells of windproof cotton or ventile are almost as good, a disadvantage being that those materials do not shed snow as readily, and therefore, are prone to wetting and freezing. However, they are cheaper and some prefer shells of these traditional materials. A wool hat or balaclava is a must, as are gloves or mitts. A good arrangement for the hands is a thin glove of polypropylene under a mitt of the Helly Hansen or Dachstein type. Waterproof/windproof overmitts are seldom necessary for alpine summers but may be needed outside that time.

A good pair of gaiters is a sensible addition. Those of canvas are more than adequate while gaiters of Gore-tex are a positive luxury. A scarf is useful for keeping the neck cosy while a silk neck-tie keeps the sun off the back of the neck − a vulnerable area − as well as lending a touch of sartorial *élan* to your ensemble. When walking on glaciers or crossing snowfields or when otherwise unhelmeted some like to cap the lot with a broad-brimmed sunhat. Others prefer to fry.

ADDITIONAL GEAR FOR BIVOUACS

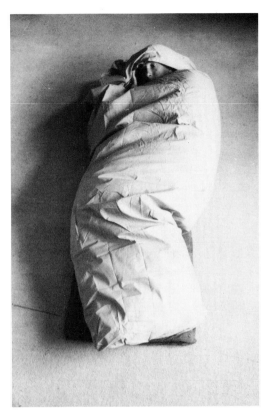

Fig 42 Bivouacking: a climber (armchair variety) snuggles in to a Gore-tex bivouac bag.

(The practicalities of bivouacking are dealt with on page 169). An alpine team should always carry some form of emergency shelter even if it is only a good-sized polythene bag, one to each, in which they can sit out unexpected storms or benightments. A modern, and better, alternative is a Gore-tex bivvi-bag which, though expensive, provides waterproof, condensation-free protection for a wide range of activities from summer hillwalking to alpine routes on the highest mountains. Cared for they'll last a lifetime; a good investment. For first seasons though, a poly bag will do well enough.

There are a number of specialist bivvi-tents designed to accommodate two or three people and equipped with guys so that they can be erected or suspended in the most unlikely places: such tents are seldom necessary on anything but the most serious of alpine routes, and even then of questionable advantage for any summer use. Ledges are not always so accommodating as to allow climbers to sleep side by side, a formation to which a bivvi-tent confines you. Individual bivouac bags allow much greater freedom and scope.

Sleeping Mat

A simple piece of closed cell foam mat (such as the ubiquitous karrimat) will make any bivouac both more comfortable and warmer for a few extra ounces of weight. Indeed, some rucksacks are padded at.the back with such a mat inserted into a sleeve so that it can be removed and replaced as necessary. For emergencies, or the one-off bivouac, the mat need be no more than torso length. For planned or regular bivouacs you should consider carrying the few extra ounces of a full length mat.

Keeping warm at night is largely a matter of personal needs and partly a matter of metabolism: some are able to blissfully snore the night away while their fellows shiver the whole night long, the both clad in identical thicknesses of insulation. There are 'warmies' and 'coldies', it seems. For involuntary summer bivouavs you'll probably get away with a poly bag and some spare clothes – pullover, balaclava, stockings – though don't expect the soundest slumber.

Sleeping Bags or Duvets?

For planned nights out there are two schools of thought – the duvet or down parka school and the sleeping bag school. And like so many things in mountaineering it is mainly a matter of what you fancy. My own

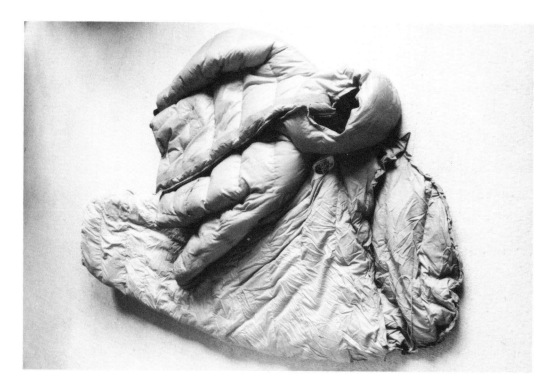

Fig 43   Duvet versus sleeping bag: there's not much to choose between them in bulk and weight.

preference is for a very light sleeping bag – there are several on the market that weigh 2lb or less. My reasons are:

1. A light bag weighs no more than a duvet and it is much warmer.
2. Although a duvet has the advantage that it can be worn on the move, in summer at least, this is a theoretical rather than a practical asset; ten steps in a duvet and the wearer is a sweating inferno. In practice duvets spend as much time in rucksacks as sleeping bags and when worn for sleep keep only half of their owner warm.
3. The same light sleeping bags can be used in the valley for camping.
4. Sleeping bags are no more expensive than duvets and even if you own a duvet, you'll still need a bag in the valley – unless you can put your legs into your pockets!

Bags and duvets may be filled with either down or a man-made synthetic fibre such as hollofil or one of that family. The pros and cons are:

Down

Pros	Cons
lighter (warmth for warmth)	expensive
warmer (weight for weight)	efficiency loss when damp
longer life time	useless when wet
more compressible	slow-drying

Man-Made Fibre

Pros	Cons
cheaper	heavier (warmth for warmth)
much less affected by damp	bulkier (weight for weight)
some insulation even when	
utterly wet	cooler (weight for weight)
	life span 5 years

In the end, 'you pays your money and takes your choice'. Very light duvets, or down-pullovers as they are sometimes called, or ski jackets make a very warm and light alternative to a spare pullover.

Stoves

A brew of tea or soup can make the worst bivouacs tolerable, the best utter delights. There's a host of suitable stoves available, the major difference really being in fuel type: gas or liquid. Gas stoves are probably the most popular for bivouacs; they are light, clean, quick to light and easy to use. After a very cold night ordinary butane gas may be sluggish. The answer is to use a butane/propane mix, if you can get it, or to keep your gas cylinders warm by sleeping with them inside your bag or duvet. If you have a stove from which partially exhausted cylinders may not be removed and therefore have to tuck up with stove *and* cylinder, *beware*. The stove is easily turned on by a

Fig 44 Various stoves, left to right: MSR, Epigas, Camping Gaz with tower stove attachment.

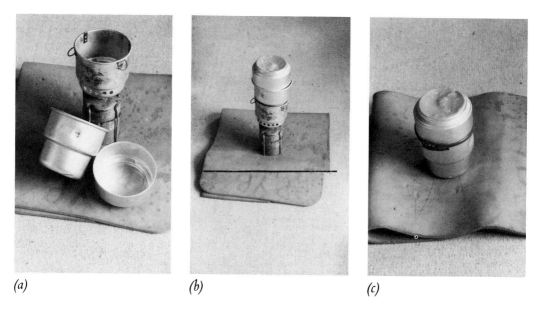

(a)   (b)   (c)

Fig 45 *A tower stove (a) demounted, (b) mounted, and (c) stowed.*

Fig 46 *Mike's Megaburner.*

restless sleeper. At least one climber has been gassed in this way. Quite a few modern gas stoves are equipped with self-sealing cylinders that may be unscrewed easily and safely, so that the cylinder can be seperated and self-sealed before you take it to your bosom.

Pans

Pans are pretty much pans. They are more efficient tall than wide and a lid saves minutes and fuel. There are a number of tower pans on the market for those who intend to make a habit (or a fetish) of bivouacking and although they are not essential they'll improve the efficiency of gas stoves, protecting against wind and enabling them to be suspended when a restricted bivouac has no kitchen floor space. I have a friend, one of those ever-practical North Country lads who specialises in improving the functional, honing perfection, who has combined the camper's Trangia, simplest of all stoves, with the MSR, hottest of all stoves, into a windproof, suspendable, unspillable, turbo-charged, barely controlled explosion, that he claims boils water in femto-seconds and the performance of which he sums up as 'mustard'. I show you a photo of it; testament to man's ingenuity (Fig 46).

CAMERAS AND PHOTOGRAPHY

Whilst a camera is hardly an essential item in the alpinist's armoury, it is certainly one worthy of consideration. Most climbers like to be able to summon up a picture and no matter how searing an image has burned through the mind's eye, it will fade in time from vivid technicolour to a sepia tint at best. But transparencies will last forever and colour prints for nearly as long. So whether you merely want pretty pictures as mementos or carefully catalogued trans-parencies with which to populate a slide library, a camera is likely to be a near constant companion.

Lightness is a major consideration. SLR cameras with interchangeable lenses give you great flexibility and artistic scope, but you pay a weight penalty. If you decide to save weight by taking only one lens then a 28 mm wide angle is probably the most useful focal length. Such a lens produces satisfactory results in most subjects, its chief advantage being that once on a route and no longer free to move about in order to frame your shot, you will still be able to get all of your partner in the frame, even though he may be fairly close. Focusing is less critical too in wide-angled lenses and this may save time – and the shot.

However, if, in order to save weight, you carry only one lens with your SLR you might as well carry – or at least consider it – a lightweight fixed lens, 35mm camera such as one of the Olympus XA series. These weigh a fraction of an SLR but to the lay eye the photographic quality, especially with colour slides, is practically indis-tinguishable from those of its bigger brother. XAs are available with 35mm and 28mm lenses. But any camera will bring you a picture and that may be the important thing.

If you're going to make a habit of carrying a camera you may as well make a habit too of keeping it handy – that is, slung over a shoulder rather than stashed away in a sack. Cameras carried in this way, however, are vulnerable to the knocks of an alpine day and so a protective case is a good thing – either the one supplied by the manufacturer, or, if you are adept at DIY, a superior shock absorbing version, home-made from neoprene.

A UV filter is a must for colour, other-wise much of your photographs will be washed over with a bluish tinge, and a polarising filter is useful for darkening skies and eliminating unwanted reflections.

In anything other than poor weather there's ample light. Indeed there may be so much reflected off the snow that you may have to take a light reading for a portrait from the end of the subject's nose in order to ensure that the metre hasn't been fooled by all that reflected light. Film speeds can, therefore, be relatively slow (and the film quality correspondingly high). For colour

slides film speeds of 25–100 ASA are fine, while for prints 100–200 ASA are suitable.

If you are restricted to one camera per team, it is worth remembering that taking two shots at every exposure is cheaper than making copies of slides – and the results are far better too.

It is a curious phenomenon that slopes and walls and faces that feel awesomely plumb to the climber look tamely innocuous once photographed. If the aim is to impress you might consider tilting the camera. Most of us do. If you do decide to gild nature in this manner make sure you tilt the camera the right way otherwise you might end up with the climber looking as if he's doing press-ups on ground not much steeper than flat instead of hanging by the fingernails on a gently overhanging nordwand as had been your intention. Generally, be cautious and conservative with your tilting – otherwise the results can rather give the game away.

GEAR FOR A CLIMB

It might be useful to look at two typical sets of gear matched to climbs of a very different order of difficulty.

Traverse of the Barre Des Ecrins (4102m)

This fine but straightforward peak in the Dauphiné Region of the French Alps is the highest in the Massif des Ecrins (*see* page 173 for a more detailed look at this route). A glacier, the Glacier Blanc, leads from a hut to a fairly easy angled snow slope. This leads to a broken rocky ridge, more of a scramble than a climb, which in turn leads to the summit. From the summit a great scramble along a ridge runs down to a brèche before

Fig 47   This photograph was used to pass on information about a new route on Mt. Cook back in 1969.

the Dôme de Neige des Ecrins. The brèche is gained by a steep scramble, or sometimes an abseil, from whence a descent down a huge, crevassed, snow basin takes the climber back down to the Glacier Blanc, the Ecrins hut and valley. In all about an 8-hour day, overall alpine grade, AD (*see* page 26 for gradings), with straightforward snow and ice work, scrambling on rock and a fine airy traverse. For a team of two:

Personal Gear

leather or plastic mountaineering boots (or those lightweight boots of which I have written earlier)
crampons
ice axe
harness
helmet
personal clothing
sunglasses
suncream
headtorch
small rucksack
prusik loops
snack
water bottle

Gear to Share

one 45m rope; 9 or 10mm
2 long slings
3 short slings
6 assorted nuts
8 karabiners
small first aid kit
map and compass

I'll use this same route again as a model, when discussing daily alpine procedure (*see* Chapter 6).

North Face of the Eiger (3970m)

For the harder route let's take the North Face of the Eiger by the 1938 route, if only because it's one that everyone will have heard of. (It's also one of the best routes in the Alps.) This route lies on a steep 1,600m wall rising from a meadow and consists of 2,000m of rock, mixed and ice climbing. Conditions vary wildly from mostly rock, to mostly ice to mostly something in between. Storms threaten and a climber's gear will reflect this. And despite the fact that several folk have climbed the route in less than a day, bivouacs are to be expected by mere mortals. The same sort of gear as you might consider deploying on the Eiger would see you up most serious alpine routes the world over. Examples might be the East Ridge of Deborah, Alaska; The Diamond Couloir, Mt. Kenya; the South Face of Hicks, New Zealand; one of the faces in the Cordillera Blanca, the 'Alps' of Peru; one of the big North Faces in the Canadian Rockies – or indeed any Himalayan face of alpine scale.

Personal Gear

helmet
ice axe, ice hammer
crampons
plastic boots
gaiters
harness, belay brake
clothing (including underwear, plenty of insulation and a Gore-tex shell for torso and legs)
spare socks, gloves inner and outer, balaclava
light sleeping bag and bivouac bag (or a warmer, and therefore heavier bag, for colder climbs) or a duvet (*see* also page 60), or take none of it and go quickly, or shiver.

65

Fig 48   The Eiger with the N. Face in shadow.

sleeping mat
sunglasses
suncream
biggish rucksack – about 55/60 litres
plastic mug, spoon
penknife
length of plastic tube – as a straw to reach
otherwise inaccessible trickles of water.

Shared Gear

2 × 50m 9mm ropes (different colours)
2 long slings
10 short slings
12 assorted nuts, friends, etc.
8 assorted pegs
6 ice screws, snargs or equivalent; lighter
the better
20 karabiners

spare tape (for abseil loops)
gas stove and spare cylinders
pan and lid
up to 3 days food and brews
small first aid kit
copy of route description and topo
compass
appropriate fragment of map

These lists of kit are not mandatory. They
are, at best, a guide. Everyone will have their
own preferences; favourite items. I know
one lad who won't go near a mountain
without a copy of the anthology, *Other
Men's Flowers* – not the most practical of
tools, though a handy spanner for the spirit;
another who insists on taking a singularly
useless First World War tin mug that
combines   the   unique   properties   of

simultaneously cooling the contents and scalding the lips; yet another who will not be seen on the mountain without a supply of marzipan and a lass who swears a certain T-shirt brings her luck and wears it the alpine season long, despite the fact that its thermal properties are non-existent and that it is now so holey that it's 'nothing much before an' rather less than 'alf o' that be'ind'. 'There's nowt so queer as folk.' If your own experience suggests a trustier kit list, then so much the better.

3 Hill Walkers' Alps

The alps, any alps, are not necessarily the exclusive preserve of mountaineers: these are great things and big adventures stretching to the earth's last horizons for hillwalkers too. Your fancy may be to roam the glaciers to breathe the air of alps, and gaze on the prospect of alps from (usually) below. Or it may be to clamber to the highest summits, albeit by an easy route say Facile, in the Vallot System (*see* page 127). As I have already said, the normal route up Mont Blanc from the French side is a walkable route – with a couple of provisos that will be dealt with shortly. The world is full of glorious summits that may be reached without recourse to technical climbing skills and a hill walker with the inclination and energy to roam the mountains should be neither dissuaded nor deterred by the welter of technicality of gear and information that is the apparent accompaniment to all things alpine. And whilst everything in this

Fig 49 Hill walkers' Alps.

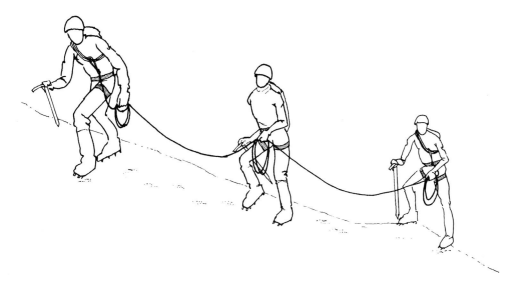

Fig 50 A team moving together, coils in hand, on easy ground.

handbook may be relevant to their desires only a few items of gear and a handful of skills are essential.

The essential gear can be summarised as:

For a group of up to 3:
rope – 40m × 9mm

Then for each:
harness (page 54)
3 prusik loops
slings (2 × 2m, 1 × 3m)
ice axe (page 41)
crampons (page 33)
boots (page 130)
daysack (c. 30 litres) (page 65, containing water bottle, map and compass, pocket knife, first aid kit, spare clothing, sunglasses, route description, food, poly survival bag)
4 lightweight karabiners – 2 screwgate, 2 snaplink

Items that might also be considered are:

helmet – depending on nature of the approaches to the route and the nature of the route itself.
stove, pot
mug – should a bivouav be intended or likely
altimeter – as an aid to navigation and to forecasting
a light-weight pulley – *see* Crevasse Escape for more details

GLACIER TRAVEL AND CREVASSE ESCAPE

These are dealt with in Chapter 4 (pages 128–148) and as a walker amongst the Alps you will need to be as conversant with them as the hardened (or not so hardened) mountineer. This is a big step from sub-alpine hills – a long one rather than a difficult one. Practise, familiarise, and practise again until you are happy that you can take coils like a python, move roped together with ease, *élan* even, and that you can escape crevasses if you fall victim, as well as being able to extricate your mates, should they fall victim.

AXES AND CRAMPONS

Walkers' Axes

All you need to know (and more) of axes has been covered in Chapter 2 (pages 41–50).

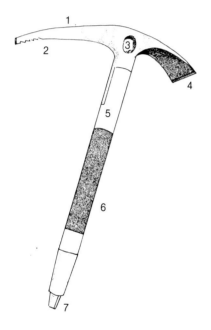

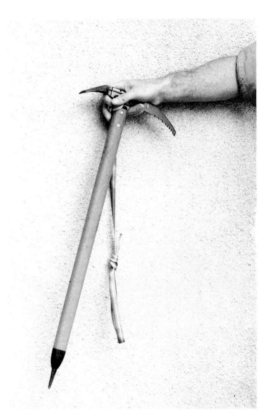

Fig 52 A simple walking axe with a homemade sling. The axe shown at Fig 25 would be an equally acceptable axe for walkers – and there are dozens of other models to choose from.

Fig 51 The ice axe.
1. The pick – should be gently curved so that it holds better.
2. A few teeth improve the bite – though there need only be a few.
3. Hole for a sling (see page 71).
4. The adze.
5. The shaft.
6. Improved grip, e.g. roughened, taped, rubberised.
7. The spike.

Choose a simple axe such as the one shown on page 41 and befriend it: play with it, on and off the ice, until it belongs to you. An axe of about 70cm in length with a slight curve or droop to the pick and adze that will cut a decent step the odd time one is needed is what you're after. Use it with a sling attached to the head and adjusted so that it is taut when the axe is held in the fist just above the spike.

It is worth summarising the pros and cons of such a sling.

 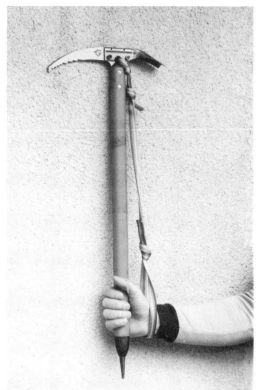

(a)   (b)

Fig 53   The sling should be tied and adjusted – which might take some fiddling – so that it is tight when the hand is holding the shaft just above the spike. Note the different ways of grasping the wrist loop. (a) consumes fractionally more tape than (b) so pre-select your preferred grasp and match the tape accordingly.

Advantages

1.   Security if the axe is dropped.
2.   Support when pulling up on the axe as when on a steep step in an otherwise easy route.
3.   Reinforces grip.
4.   Can be dropped to dangle on wrist, freeing the hand for other purposes.

Disadvantages

1.   Can cause entanglement when self-arresting.

2.   If let go in a tumble it may bang the owner about the body. (Moral – don't let go.)
3.   Changing hands on every zigzag means re-inserting the wrist into wrist loop.

These disadvantages notwithstanding, a wrist loop is generally a useful thing. It need not be engaged on a zigzagging ascent, or if it proves irksome it may be allowed to dangle harmlessly along the shaft as in Fig 52. It is, furthermore, a very simple business to manufacture a quickly removable wrist

Fig 54   It is a simple matter to make a sling that is easy to remove.

loop and then you have the best of both worlds.

Using the Axe

In practice, axe and crampons are seldom divorced, except on glaciers where an axe will always be to hand and where crampons, on flattish glaciers at least, may be dispensed with. Once on the mountain, however, the two (or three really) are complementary.

The Axe on Gentle Slopes

On very easy ground carry the axe as you please. Indeed, it may be that it remains attached to your rucksack. On moderate slopes the axe can be used as a kind of third leg: hold it by the head, always in the uphill hand where it will be nearer to the snow, and use it for support. There are those who spend happy hours arguing whether, when the axe is used in this way, the pick should face forwards or backwards. It matters not. One may prove more comfortable than the other, or you may decide that one is the more natural position from which to perform self-arrest. Try both and take your choice. If you can find no reason to discriminate then it is suggested that you make a habit of carrying the axe with the pick pointing backwards. That way, should you slip, the pick will be in a ready position. Try it; I think the argument will soon be clear. It is not always necessary (or desirable) to don crampons at the first sniff of a snow slope, though crampons nearly always afford an advantage on ice of any angle.

Without crampons steps can be kicked in crusty snow and soft névé just as you would kick a football, and for hours on end, with the axe for support in your uphill hand and ready to be deployed in self-arrest if need be. When kicking steps, a lazy rhythm will make life easier. Those following should use the same steps and enjoy the ride. As long as a reasonable kick produces a step deep enough to accommodate a third of the boot it makes perfectly good sense to proceed in this way. If, because of the hardness of the snow, you are only able to lodge an inch or so, life will probably be easier wearing crampons. Safety and economy of effort are the two considerations – weigh them and decide. Sometimes it's a toss-up, but no matter.

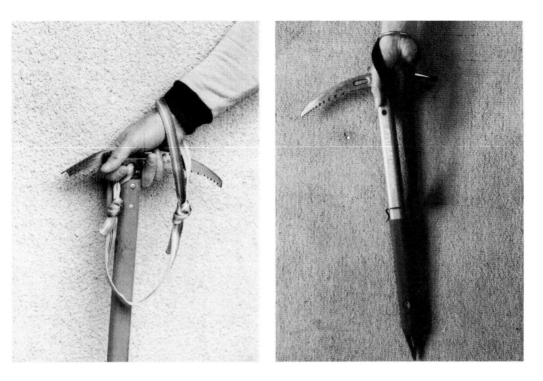

Fig 55 *'Hold it by the head, always in the uphill hand'.*

Fig 56 *Kicking steps: maintain balance and rhythm.*

Step-Cutting

'To cut a step in ice is obviously uncomplicated, and you can fashion it to suit your own taste – soup plates for big feet and mantelshelfing, or "God save all here" jug handles. It is an art form, and self-expression is rare indeed in mountaineering. It only becomes a mountaineering skill when you have the ability to cut a few gross or to do without when there isn't enough ice. However, this approach is only applicable to the historic romantic period which prevailed before the sixties, for the last decade has "done for" the bold, committed leads of bygone days, when the knickerbocker brigade would lead up a hundred feet of ice secured only by a dessicated old ice-axe belay.' (Jimmy Marshall in *Mountain*.)

73

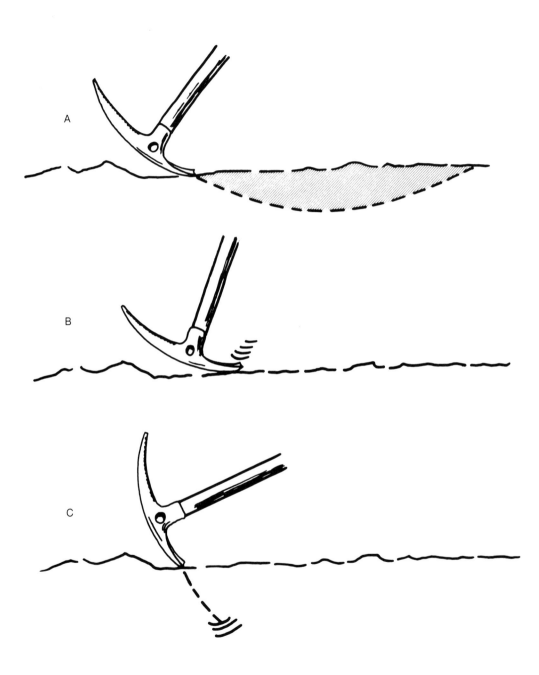

*Fig 57 Cutting a step.   A: about the right angle; B: too shallow a
swing results in a glancing blow and wasted energy; C: too steep a swing
results in an embedded axe and more wasted energy.*

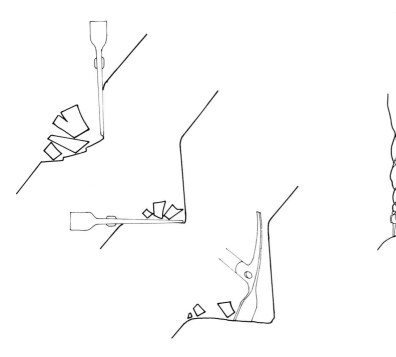

Fig 58   Chopping a step to rest on, or as a stance from which to prepare a belay. Ensure you use the whole step – this gives you greater security and leaves the edge of the step intact for those following.

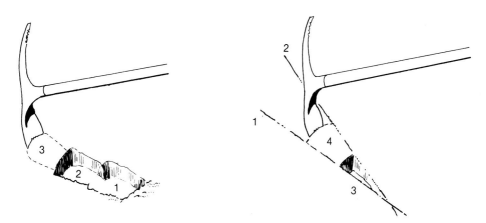

Fig 59   In slabby snow, make two slashes (1 and 2) with the pick and then chop out the angle between them with the adze (3 and 4). With the adze, always chop away from the first cut.

Traditionalists will be dismayed that I have reduced the noble art of step-cutting, once a subject deemed worthy of years of apprenticeship, and deserving of an entire chapter, to a mere section, sulking under a subheading. That I believe to be its proper fate. Climbing moves on. Today's crampons and axes have largely – though by no means wholly – left step-cutting (and step-cutters) to history. For those few times when it is prudent to cut a step, however, it is certainly worth studying how best this is done.

Shallow, though not too shallow, blows are the most efficient. Blows that are too steeply angled merely become embedded in the ice and energy is wasted in extraction. Swing the axe from the shoulder, with a loosely straight arm, rather than from the elbow with a bent arm – the first is much less strenuous and much more efficient.

A step on a steep ice pitch can provide a welcome rest; one foot on is usually enough. Steps will also make an uncomfortable belay stance more amenable.

Walking in Crampons

Volumes have been written about the business of climbing with crampons – some of it good, some of it unnecessary, some of it turning a fairly straightforward skill into a black art, and some of it mumbo-jumbo. It is my considered advice that the best way to learn how to use crampons is to put them on and to go out and play with them: on the flat, on easy slopes, on short, steeper slopes and on very short, very steep slopes; up, down, sideways left and sideways right, diagonally left and right and every which way. Play until you are as at home with your crampons on ice as you would be in carpet slippers on a rug. Play

until you have exhausted the process of discovery of what the front-points will do, what the down-points will do, how steep you can go without hands and how steep with hands. Have some fun. It will take a few minutes, perhaps a few hours, before they no longer feel strange. Keep at it until you can dance a jig on a 40-degree slope, and then you'll be ready to climb in your crampons. You may trip or fall – it doesn't matter in a safe place.

The following points are distilled from all that might be said about climbing with crampons. You may hear of a French technique (which isn't half as exciting as it sounds), and a German technique – almost everyone, it seems, claims to have invented a technique. Ignore all the names – it is only the method that matters. The problem is that the French think they invented the art of using crampons (which they probably did) and have been bent on inflicting their code on the rest of the climbing world ever since. The Germans think they re-invented it all (which they probably did) and have been bent on doing everything better and faster then the French (which they don't). As Chouinard comments in *Climbing on Snow and Ice*:

'The sixties were the age of super-nationalism in alpine sports. This was especially true in skiing, where there were Austrian, French and even American techniques. The French, with their 10-point crampons, were artfully angling and flat-footing their way up to the big snow faces of the Mont Blanc range, while the Austrians and Germans were tiptoeing around on only their front-points. In 1969 the leading spokesman for ice climbing in France, André Contamine, wrote in the journal *La Montagne*: "The *piolet ancre* is one of the most useful techniques of the alpinist. It permits him to cover ground on the steepest slopes without fatigue or difficulty. It is the key to cramponing French style". Two years later the Austrian climber, Wastl Mariner, wrote in the same journal: "The most natural technique anatomically, and the most secure and sparing of energy, is to advance on steep ice on the front-points of 12-point crampons – called front-pointing." He went on to criticise the French technique for being unnatural and difficult to learn. This caused an absolute furore at the Ecole National de Ski et Alpinism in Chamonix, when rebellious students posted the article on the bulletin board!'

It seems more sensible not to worry about such arcana as *pied assis* or *en canard* (unless you know what a duck is) and to do what comes easiest and most naturally – fore-armed with a little reading and rearmed with a little experience.

Donning Crampons

Stories of competent climbers getting half-way up a route before attempting to put on crampons on some ridiculously steep slope or exiguous ledge are legion. Put crampons on whilst still on easy ground – you will seldom regret it, and if you do you can always take them off again. If they have modern step-in bindings, putting them on is easy. Lay them on the ground, or snow if it presents a firm surface, or a rock or a rucksack if it doesn't, and push the toe wire forward and the heel clip back. Step in. Locate the toe wire in the welt of the boot. Place the heel piece on the welt at the heel and lever into position. Correctly fitted, it should click into position with a suggestion

of a snap. Step-in bindings don't have to be very tight and it should take no perceptible effort to snap the heel piece home. This done, fasten the safety strap around the ankle, repeat the operation on the other foot, give them both a good shake, check them visually – and away you go.

Life is not much more complicated with more conventional straps. Lay crampons on a firm surface, position all rings and straps outboard of posts, step in, fasten front straps, fasten angle straps, and check. Away you go.

Crampon Techniques

1. *Easy Ground*. Walk more or less as normal. You'll soon become accustomed to being an inch or so taller and to your boot soles being effectively an inch or so deeper. Remember that you have ten downward-facing points – the more points you are able to use, the greater security you gain. Instead

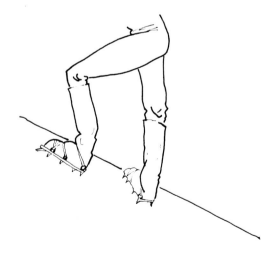

Fig 60 Doing what comes naturally on easy to moderate ground. The important thing is that all the points are working.

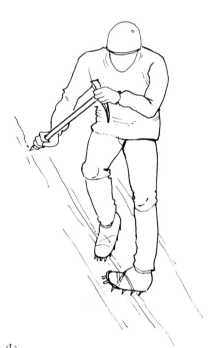

(a)   *(b)*

Fig 61(a) Climbing on a moderately steep slope with axe and crampons. The axe is in the uphill hand, the ankles are rolled out so that the feet are inclined with the slope, and – the important bit, however it is achieved – all downward points are engaged with the snow or ice. (b) When the going gets steeper it may be more comfortable to brace with the axe.

of edging feet, as you would naturally in boots without crampons, allow your ankles to roll out from the slope so that the soles of your boots lie at the same angle as the slope and all ten points are encouraged to bite.

2. *Moderate ground: slopes up to 55 degrees.* Going up doing what comes naturally in these circumstances means using the feet flat on the ground. Because of the ground's angle, this entails placing the feet across the foot. Try it – it's not nearly as difficult as it sounds. Clearly the ice-axe plays a big part on the ground of intermediate and beyond. Its function will be explained shortly.

3. *Traversing.* Simply walk or climb sideways, feet still flat and encouraging all down points to bite by rolling the ankle of the outboard foot pronouncedly outwards. If you lack flexibility in the ankles, you may find traversing easier if you point the toe of the lower foot downhill, with the foot still flat on the slope. As the slope steepens, both feet will tend to point downhill. If this feels natural, use them both that way.

4. *Climbing down.* It is quicker (and after practice, easier) to continue to face outwards for as long as nerve and angle allow – and both should allow up to 50 degrees or so. On your first day at play on safe snow slopes and ice boulders it is worth

78

Fig 62 Rolling the ankles out so all down-points bite.

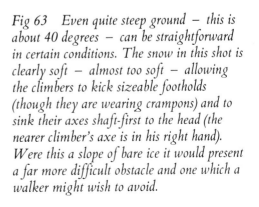

practising descents facing outwards. You will probably surprise yourself at the steepness of slopes that can be safely and quickly negotiated in this way. But it does take practice, especially on hard ice.

You will soon discover that in order to have all ten down-points working you have to sit back; and that the steeper the slope, the more pronounced this squat will be. Play with the axe too and discover all the ways that it can help you, from being placed spike down, hand on axe head, walking stick-like below or to the side; to being held, hand in sling, and hooked (by the pick) behind on steeper steps. When you are no longer

Fig 63 Even quite steep ground − this is about 40 degrees − can be straightforward in certain conditions. The snow in this shot is clearly soft − almost too soft − allowing the climbers to kick sizeable footholds (though they are wearing crampons) and to sink their axes shaft-first to the head (the nearer climber's axe is in his right hand). Were this a slope of bare ice it would present a far more difficult obstacle and one which a walker might wish to avoid.

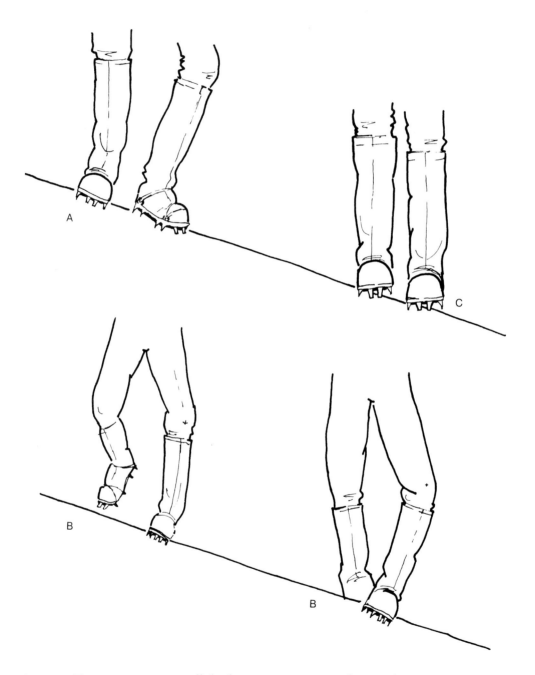

Fig 64 Traversing: encourage all the down-points to engage the snow by turning the foot downhill as in A, or by rolling the ankles outwards as in B. C is poor technique and only half of the points are working.

Sarah Bishop cruises on the South Ridge (Promontoire) of the Meije, a classic AD in the Dauphiné Alps.

Moving together near the top of the Yokum Ridge, Mt. Hood, Oregon, USA, ropework temporarily abandoned!

A climber poses contra jour *on the summit of the Aiguille de Tour, Chamonix. Photo: Nigel Shepherd.*

*On the Midi/Plan traverse above Chamonix, a classic alpine traverse
(PD). Photo: Nigel Shepherd.*

Dave Walsh on his way to the Glacier Blanc hut in the Dauphiné.
Behind from left to rise the triple summits of the Pelvoux; the Pic
Sans Nom and the Ailfroide.

Two lads, tired but exhilarated, nearing the summit of Mont Pelvoux,
Dauphiné Alps.

On a dry(ish) glacier in front of the southern flank of the Barre des Ecrins, Dauphiné Alps. The ropework and the method by which the rope has been shortened is not above criticism; nor any crampons — yet.

The Matterhorn; quintessential alp. The Hörnli hut can be discerned on the rocky ridge that joins the pinnacle above the climber to the mountain.

On the South Face of the Gletschorn (Grauwand) in traditional alpine garb. This is a fine sunny climb (about VS) on superb rock, which lends itself readily to the modern 'cragrat' approach.

A newer, lighter approach to the South Face of the Gletschorn; the author shod in lightweight rock boots and sans sack — a reasonable risk on 1,500 ft of VS climbing where the descent is straightforward and sub-alpine; that is no glacier.

Terry Storry on the traverse of the Aiguilles Dorées, Chamonix.
Photo: Nigel Shepherd.

Near the summit of Pic Coolidge with the Ailefroide behind, Dauphiné
Alps.

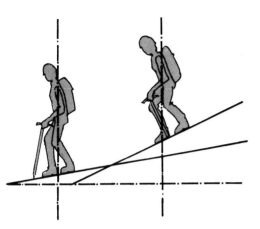

Fig 65   As the ground steepens, sit back over your heels so that all your crampon points are biting.

Fig 66   On moderately steep ground it is still possible to descend facing outwards – which is quicker – by sitting in a pronounced crouch.

(a)

(b)

Fig 67   (a) and (b): Descending ice.

(a)   (b)

Fig 68   (a) Traversing on ice; (b) Climbing with one walking axe.

comfortable descending facing out it is time to turn in to the slope.

SELF-ARREST AND GLISSADING

Some may consider the pairing of self-arrest (or ice-axe breaking) and glissading to be inappropriate. The pessimists will point out that glissading too often makes a necessity of self-arrest and that it is the province of experts. The weakness in this argument is that it admits no way of becoming an expert. The killjoys, and even so joyous a game as winter climbing is burdened with a few, claim that glissading is dangerous and should not be practised at all. Rationally,

this argument makes little sense to me, in view of the nature of mountaineering, whilst practically, it disavows a safe and efficient method of losing height – given the right circumstances. It is perhaps wise to look at self-arrest first.

Self-Arrest

If you are already a winter hillwalker you will be familiar with this series of skills, and aware of the importance of proficiency in them. Even the most experienced mountaineers sometimes slip on snow or ice, and a slip can accelerate alarmingly into a wildly out of control fall, especially if the unfortunate is dressed in smooth-surfaced waterproof clothing, as is likely. To be able be too late. Choose a concave slope or one with a long, safe run out so that friction will stop you if you fail to stop yourself. Avoid boulders.

In the basic braking position, you lie face to the slope, one hand on the head of the axe with the adze tucked hard in against chest and shoulder and the pick pressed hard to the slope. The other hand holds the axe shaft somewhere near the spike. Some advocate holding the spike itself, so that it cannot pierce the torso if things go wrong. This is worth considering. Hunch the body over the axe. Falls on steep ground will call for all the weight and strength you can muster, so keep your legs splayed for stability, and apply that weight and effort to the pick gradually. Too sudden an effort may result in the pick biting abruptly and the axe being snatched from your grasp. If you are wearing crampons, lift your feet from the snow. If they snag at speed they will cause you to tumble. Don't practise with crampons on – they add unnecessary difficulty to an already tricky matter. However, practise as if you are wearing crampons; it breeds good habits.

Should you find yourself tumbling after a slip, spread-eagle with arms and legs. This will stop the tumble. Then apply the braking technique appropriate to the attitude in which you find yourself post-tumble. Rucksack and crampons, both of which you are likely to be wearing when a real fall occurs, serve to complicate matters. Since, in my own experience at any rate, real falls are always much faster and more furious than practice falls, it behoves you to invest some hours in self-arrest. The skill and effort needed to stop a slide should not be taken lightly. Speed of reaction may be vital. Note that in the Alps you may well be roped-up when you slip. With any luck

Fig 69   The braking position, viewed from the snow. The shaded areas show the parts of the body most likely to be in contact with the snow.

to stop, and to stop quickly, is important – sometimes crucial. Under ideal conditions and on gentle slopes the necessary techniques are not too difficult to master. Unfortunately, slips seldom occur under such friendly circumstances, and a tumble on a 30-degree ice slope takes some stopping. As in all things, practise, practise and practise again is the key – and practise early in your ice climbing career. Later may

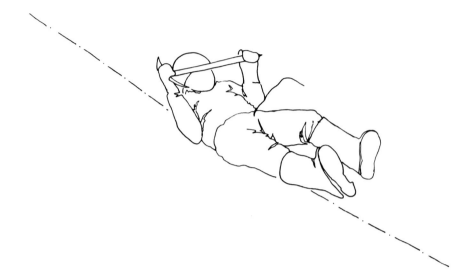

Fig 70   A feet-first fall.

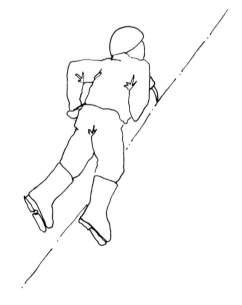

Fig 71   Rolling into the braking position following a feet-first fall. Roll towards the hand that is holding the axe-head and apply pressure with pick gradually so that the axe is not snatched from your grasp.

Fig 72   It is advisable to keep your feet off the snow surface when applying the brake, unless it is very soft snow.

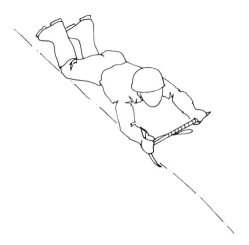

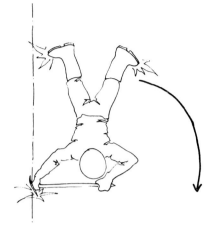

Fig 73   Braking after a head-first fall, face down. Head-first falls are more difficult to control and the first action is to get into a head-uphill position. From here the conventional self-arrest technique can be used.

Fig 74   Falling head-first face down, reach out horizontally with the pick as far as you can on the same side as the arm which is holding the axe-head. Bring the pick to the snow and the braking effect on that side will cause you body to swing round past the axe into a head-uphill position.

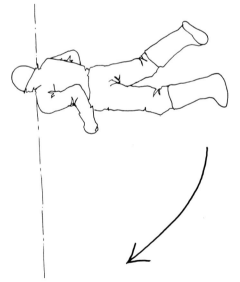

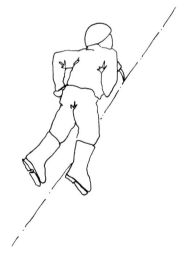

Fig 75   You will now have your arms at full stretch, so arch your back upwards, lift out the pick and place it below your shoulder to brake as before.

Fig 76   The final braking position.

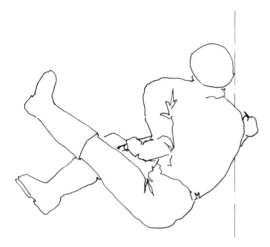

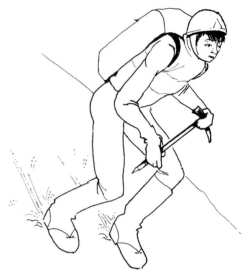

Fig 77 A head-first fall on your back: (a) Insert the pick close to your hip and on the same side as the arm which is holding the axe-head. (b) Dig the pick in and at the same time pull yourself into a sitting position. (c) Bring your knees up towards your chest, then swing your legs away from the axe-head and allow them to fall through into a position with your head uphill, from which a normal arrest can be made.

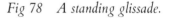

Fig 78 A standing glissade.

your partner(s) will arrest your slide. However, in the worst case you will pull them all with you: this is where self-arrest becomes a collective responsibility; a corporate task to be tackled with a will. Nor will the presence of ropes and a (perhaps) heavy sack make matters any easier.

Glissading

Glissading is enormous fun and a very quick and efficient way of losing height. It can, however, be dangerous. Common sense is the key. There are two methods: standing and sitting. The standing glissade is the harder to perfect, but probably the more comfortable once mastered. The position

Fig 79 The bum slide.

and execution of a standing glissade are akin to those of skiing, although your skis are only as long as your feet. Position the body as far forward as is necessary to keep your weight directly over your feet, which should be flat on the snow. Keep your feet comfortably apart and parallel, hands wide for balance, and axe at the ready for a self-arrest, should your glissading fail to convey you to the bottom of the slope with the grace of a thousand startled gazelles. Turn simply by turning the feet whilst keeping the weight over the outside/lower foot, just the same as skiing.

The sitting glissade's only advantage is that you are closer to the slope when a fall does occur. It is no easier to perform and will almost certainly lead very quickly to a straightforward (and very practical) bum slide. Quite why the bum slide should be the subject of such opprobrium in the eyes of 'professional' mountaineers, instructors, guides and the like is not clear. It is a safe, speedy and foolproof way to descend – *under the right circumstances*. And the right circumstances, as with glissading are:

1.   It is safer on a slope that you know, or that you can see the bottom of. The slope should also be avalanche and obstacle (boulder) free. A good run out forgives errors.
2.   Watch out for changes in surface texture – soft snow to ice will result in dramatic acceleration.
3.   Stay in control.
4.   Keep your axe at the ready as a brake.
5.   Expect some wear to the seat of your pants – and possibly your backside as well!

4 Special Alpine Considerations

Climbing in the alps – by which is traditionally meant the Alps of Europe but by logical extension means any mountains where those conditions special to alpine areas are manifest, is a more serious business than climbing in non-alpine or sub-alpine hill areas. This chapter deals with those things, special to alps regions, that make alpinism different and more serious. Perhaps the greatest of these is the glacier – a phenomenon, with problems and solutions that have been accorded a section of their own at the end of this chapter; a position inversely proportional to importance perhaps.

SEASONS

Most alpine areas around the world are governed by climbing seasons – those months when the weather is customarily the most propitious. For example, the summer season for the European Alps is held to be between June and September; for Kenya it is December to February or July to September; for Alaska it is June/July; for Peru, May to July; for New Zealand (summer) December to March, and so on. Fig 80 shows the widely accepted seasons for the major alpine regions of the world, though it is not quite as simple as that.

A closer look at the generally accepted season for the European Alps suggests that in the early part of the season – up to mid-July say – the snow and ice climbs are in good condition, turning to unfriendly black ice some time after that; whereas rock faces are usually clear of snow from mid-July onwards and stay in 'nick' until September. There are, however, as many years that are exceptions to this very general timetable as there are years that conform. Bad seasons outnumber good seasons, and in some really bad seasons the big climbs may never come into condition at all. A high north-facing rock route, for example, that has not cleared of snow by mid-July is unlikely to clear in the remainder of the summer, no matter how sunny is August.

The volume of snow preceding winter and the earliness or lateness of the arrival of spring are also factors that play havoc with our general timetable. And to show just how general it is I have climbed rock routes on warm dry rock in May and ice routes of coruscating névé in September. Moreover, routes, and big routes too, have been climbed in October and April, months that belong neither to the traditional summer season nor to the traditional alpine winter season defined (rather arbitrarily) as 21 December to 21 February (see Winter Alps, page 184).

There are, however, few seasons so bad that, in the space of a three-week holiday, no routes are possible. Determination and some cunning usually combine to cheat the very worst of summers. If it is a snowy season concentrate on snow and ice routes – once the snow has had a chance to consolidate. Or, if you must do a rock route, try one of a southerly or south-westerly

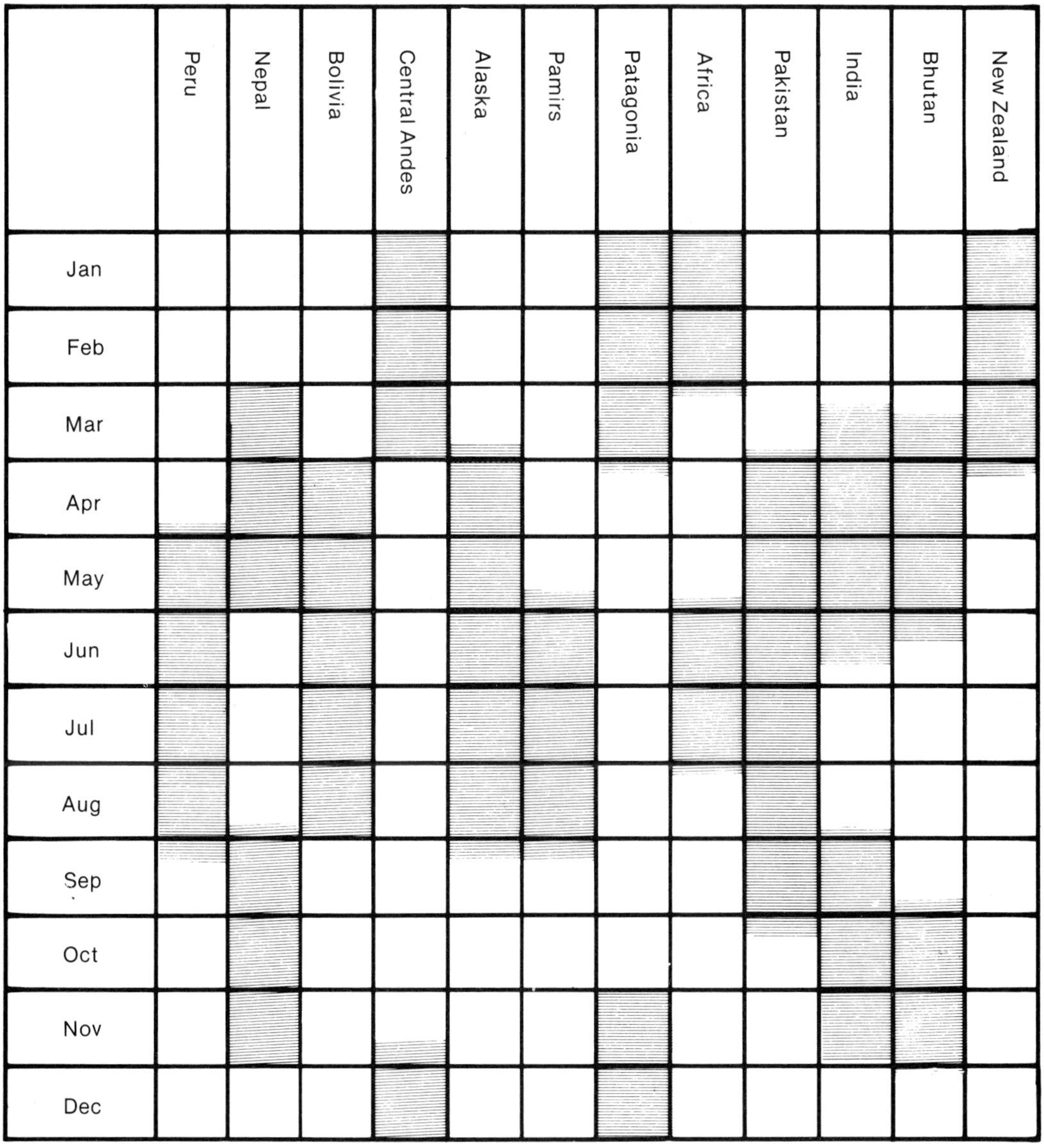

	Peru	Nepal	Bolivia	Central Andes	Alaska	Pamirs	Patagonia	Africa	Pakistan	India	Bhutan	New Zealand
Jan				▓			▓	▓				▓
Feb				▓			▓					▓
Mar		▓		▓			▓			▓	▓	▓
Apr		▓	▓		▓				▓	▓	▓	
May	▓	▓	▓		▓				▓	▓	▓	
Jun	▓		▓		▓		▓		▓	▓	▓	
Jul	▓		▓		▓		▓		▓			
Aug	▓		▓		▓		▓		▓			
Sep	▓	▓			▓				▓			
Oct		▓							▓		▓	
Nov		▓	▓	▓			▓			▓	▓	
Dec				▓			▓					

Fig 80   Climbing seasons around the world. These are approximate; the seasons for India, Pakistan and Nepal vary according to the precise area.

89

aspect – they'll clear the quickest. Try, too, to get in step with the rhythm of the weather. Even in bad seasons a spell of foul weather is often followed by two or three days of good. Be up at the hut or on the start line poised and ready to go at the first hint of improvement (and remember that ridge routes are usually safer than other sorts of route after bad weather).

Big routes will usually take a day or two to settle into climbable conditions after a storm but it will often be possible to do something even if it is fairly modest. A route after all is a route and in your early days at least almost everything is good experience. It takes some will-power to drag a reluctant body from the valley when the weather is less than perfect: valley festering is wonderfully addictive and before too long you'll be finding every excuse under the sun not to climb, and before much longer the excuses will be literally under the sun and you'll be missing climbing days and losing routes.

There is nothing so pleasant as a rest well earned by a couple of hard days on the hill, but in uncertain conditions rests all too easily degenerate (which I hope is not too perjorative a word) into festers, and festers into routeless seasons. Fester by all means, but beware.

ALPINE WEATHER

In *One Man's Mountains*, Tom Patey has an anecdote or two in a chapter entitled 'The Art of Climbing Down Gracefully'. Tom offers a 'Symposium of Commonly Used Ploys' for not climbing that day, for prolonging the fester. One such alpine ploy runs:

'The Föhn Wind and Other Bad Weather Ploys'

'Writes Réné Desmaison with spine-chilling candour, "I have heard it said that it takes more courage to retreat than to advance. I cannot share these sentiments!" M. Desmaison is of course a Frenchman writing for Frenchmen, but he would scarcely get away with this sort of remark in the *British Alpine Journal*. Not by a long chalk. It strikes at the very foundations of British alpinism and undermines our most deep-rooted traditional ploy – "Giving the Mountain Best".

'It was during my first Alpine season that I came into contact with the ever-popular Zermatt gambit. An elderly gentleman, wearing knickerbockers and armed with alpenstock, would totter out on to his hotel balcony, raising aloft one pre-moistened, trembling finger.

"Aha! – I thought as much," he would chuckle grimly. "The föhn wind is in the offing! No climbing for you, young fellow, for a week at least!"

'I was a bit frustrated by this and the next time I went up to a hut I determined to follow the advice of local alpine guides. If they don't know, who does? Thirty-two guides slept at the Couvercle Hut that night, and they all got up at 2 a.m. like a major volcanic eruption. One guide, with an attractive female client in tow, walked out, prodded the snow with an ice-axe, sniffed the night air, and without a word retired to his bed. It later transpired that this was the celebrated X.X. Thirty-one silent guides looked at each other, shook their heads, and retired likewise. We woke at 8 a.m. to find brilliant sunshine.

"Pourquoi?" I demanded wrathfully of one, "Pourquoi?" (It was one of the few

French words at my disposal, so I used it twice.)

"X.X. a dit!" he said reverently, mentally crossing himself, "C'est trop dangereux!"

"Pourquoi?" I demanded again, not without reason.

"X.X. a dit!" he repeated, waving his arms towards a cloudless horizon, "Tempête de neige, qui va venir bientôt sans doute."

'The last time I saw X. X. he was heading for the valley with the attractive blonde in close attendance. It was the first day of what proved to be a ten-day record heat wave. I remembered the time-honoured Victorian advice, "Follow the Old Guide – he knows best!" There was more than a grain of truth in that statement...

'In the hands of a reliable weather-lore expert the Bad Weather ploy can be practically infallible. Such a man can spend an entire Alpine season without setting boot to rock, simply by following the bad weather around, and consistently turning up in the wrong place at the wrong time.'

In the alps the weather is as important as it is difficult to predict. Bad weather will make any route less pleasant, most routes unpleasant and some impossible, or, at least, inadvisable. At high altitudes heavy snow, wind, hail and severe cold, all characteristic results of bad weather, are extremely unpleasant, and often dangerous. A storm will usually leave a rock climb wreathed in snow, ice and verglas and in such conditions even retreat may be hazardous, never mind advance. Deep, new snow is not only exhausting to furrow through, it can be dangerous (*see* page 99). Mist and thick, low cloud make movement on even the most straightforward ground an uncertain business and on glaciers a worrying one.

Fortunately, bad weather in alpine regions takes time to develop. In the European Alps you might expect up to six hours warning, though there are alpine regions where the time between signal and onset may be much shorter. This is certainly the case where mountains rise immediately from oceans, Mt. Cook of the Southern Alps of New Zealand and Mt. Logan in Canada are good (that is bad) examples.

It is said that some mountains make their own weather and this seems to be true of high, isolated peaks which are sometimes battered by private storms when all around is calm, sweetness and light. The Eiger, for example, enjoys (if that is the right word) a micro-climate of its own and to some extent the Matterhorn too. Experience will help you discern what is local or 'private' weather and what is more general and, therefore, more significant. You should make allowances for the following factors.

Wind Direction

Any alpine region is largely at the mercy of the wind direction and in different regions winds will warn of different things.

In Europe a wind from the north or north-east is usually a good sign heralding cold, settled weather. A wind from the west (the prevailing direction) promises less settled weather and if it blows for a period of days is often a bad sign – though not necessarily immediately so – so don't go scuttling from the hill at the first breath of a western zephyr. A warm wind from the south is almost always bad (*see* Tom Patey's synopsis on page 90). So warm southerly winds (the föhn of Switzerland or the sirocco of France and Italy) mean that the snow's surface warmed by the day, doesn't freeze at night which in turn means lousy snow climbing conditions and avalanche-prone snow on critical slopes (*see* page 99).

Clouds: Shape and Altitude

Traces of clouds speeding in from the south or west and developing as they pass over the higher summits are a positive sign that bad weather is on the way. So are stationary black clouds temporarily forming on summits; dark, hammer-headed thunder-clouds too. Solid cirrus is also a bad sign, especially if it develops and thickens into cirrostratus or altostratus. Cumulus that is developing is a bad sign; dissipating cumulus a good sign. Don't worry too much about the odd afternoon cumulus, a harmless phenomenon: fair-weather cumulus is almost bound to form over mountain masses by mid-afternoon. Moving valley cloud and valley mist can usually be discounted; it will probably clear when the sun rises.

Haze is a good sign; clear distant views usually mean that rain or snow is on the way – or has just occurred. Cold, clear nights are good; warm cloudy nights (discussed further on page 97), not so good. Some mountains betray their own characteristic tell-tale signs of bad weather. Mont Blanc, for instance, wears a distinctive cowl of cloud – white, dense and curving over menacingly. And it is no idle threat. Three times I have seen it and every time within three or four hours I've been engulfed in a

Fig 81   Clouds tumbling between alps.

Fig 82   Mont Blanc's humpty-backed cloud; a portent of bad weather.

storm. The last of those storms taught me several lessons at the same time, as recounted in *The Great Climbing Adventure*:

'I had arrived in Chamonix at Christmas alone and too late. The weather was good and everyone was out on the hill. I cast about for a partner – and finding none decided that conditions were too good to waste; it would have to be a solo, something not too serious, not too hard. The Swiss Route on the North Face of the Courtes fitted the bill perfectly; a down-hill ski approach after using the *téléphérique*, across a straightforward glacier, a cosy hut, easy to the route, a route I knew from a summer ascent, a way off I thought I could handle on

my own and without the need of a rope. Then the perfect end of this perfect day – a downhill ski home.

And that's how it went until near the end.

I regained the glacier, after a satisfying day, at about 4 pm. A storm was brewing (I had seen the tell-tale clouds from the top), the weather worsening by the minute. By the time I found the Argentière Hut a blizzard was blowing full hooligan and it was dark. The simple thing to do was to spend the night in the perfect safety of the hut, then ski down the next day – or whenever the weather allowed. There was ample grub around the shelves to survive on. But life isn't simple. I knew that just down the glacier and around the corner the lights of Chamonix were twinkling, while at the Bar Nash all sorts of delights awaited. The temptation was too much. Besides the hut was a spooky place. I mounted skis and set off by head torch. The terrain was flattish, the skiing would have been easy in normal conditions but a rucksack filled with bits for winter, a howling blizzard and a weakish lamplight ensured that it was pretty grim. An early fall put paid to the lamp's problem. In the struggle to my feet I lost it altogether. It wouldn't be found. I considered turning back, would have turned back if I had thought that I could re-find the hut. I didn't think I could and continued by map and compass.

My big worry was an ice fall over which the glacier tumbled a mile or so further down. It lay right across my path; I would have to turn left some way before it. Here I would meet a marked piste run, with poles, ski-tracks, moguls and soon a *téléphérique* station and a café; warmth and safety not much more than a mile away. I fell now more often than I skied. What in daylight would have been a ten-minute schuss was fast becoming a monument to incompetence. I was unhappy. The icefall loomed large in my imagination; I mustn't go down the glacier too far; I must pick up the poles and piste; I couldn't miss them. Surely not?

I'd missed them, I'd blown it. This was it. I was falling. Floating through space and darkness. These were the wages of bright-lights foolishness. But a quick, and not very painful crash, told me that this was not the icefall; or maybe only the beginning of it. I was in a crevasse. Blind gropings told me that. I pondered. It was as a good place to spend a night as any, comparatively sheltered and snowily soft. The hut would

have been better, Chamonix better still, but since neither was available, this would do. The sleeping bag, which I entered in company of a blast of spindrift, brought warmth and soon, sleep.

'The sky! I could see the sky. It was ten-thirty. What a place to oversleep. I packed and addressed myself to the problem of escape. This would be a big fight, the good fight. I steeled myself, braced myself. Tried to think what Messner would have done; set my jaw accordingly, screwed courage to the sticking place, strapped crampons the extra hole, wound both axes tight, Yes Sir! I stood square, Marciano square, to the crevasse wall, hunched in determination, and raised an axe with sacrificial deliberateness. Then it occurred, in the accidental way these things do, that it might be worth a look farther along to see what might lie around the corner. I advanced, axes held low and wide, OK Corral style, a few steps to where a tight squeeze allowed me round a corner. Another step and I stood blinking, bathed in warm winter sunshine, the wide open ski piste before me and a hundred holiday skiers swooping all around, Attila before Rome, Tamerlane before Samarkand, Ghengis Khan before all China. I felt a fool and overdressed. And must have looked it, all girded in crampons, double boots, overgaiters, Gore-tex suit, axes, balaclava and helmet while casually elegant punters swept by all silk, sun-glasses and Ambre Solaire. I fled to the sanctuary of the crevasse before I was seen by one of the skiers standing about gossiping, enjoying a spot of sun. Back at my bivouac I stripped off every shred of mountain apparel, packed every incriminating item into the sack, adopted as recreational an appearance as my wardrobe would allow and skied, as casually as I could, on to the piste and into the sun.

Fifteen unsteady minutes later I was sipping coffee at the *téléphérique* station – with a heightened sense of the ridiculous.

> 'O wad some Pow'r the giftie gie us
> To see oursels as others see us!
> It wad frae mony a blunder free us
> An' foolish notion.''

I'm a slow learner, but I won't be caught a fourth.

The trouble with attempting your own interpretations from such as clouds is that it tends to be a classic case of a little learning being a dangerous thing; an imperfect understanding results in an imperfect interpretation and a prognostication that might send you in high reverse back to valley or hut when, in fact, the day was set fair.

On the whole it is better to rely on the meteorologists' forecast, though even they sometimes get it wrong. In time you'll be able to temper one with the other and get the best of all worlds – which means still getting it wrong sometimes! In the case of your humpty-backed cloud over Mont Blanc, I wouldn't demur, not after three forced bivouacs. That's experience.

A good aneroid can be useful in forecasting imminent depressions or other factors that are likely to affect the weather, as long as you can understand the instrument and the signals it gives you.

Only experience will enable you to fully understand alpine weather – and even then you'll be wrong at odd times. Many alpine valley bases will post a weather forecast. These vary from simple indications at tourist offices, to simplified synopses at some climbing stores (such as Toni Gobbi's in Courmayeur) to full-blown, detailed synopses like the one posted daily outside the Guides Bureau in Chamonix. Forecasts are also available from newspapers and in many countries by telephone, though language, or lack of it, may be a problem with these sources. This chart will help in decoding the salient sections of European weather charts.

English	German	French	Italian
Air Mass	Luftmasse	Masse d'air	Massa d'aria
Anticyclone	Antizyklone, Hochdruckgebiet, Hoch	Zone de haute pression	Anticiclone, Zona di alta pressione
Climate	Kilma	Climat	Clima
Cloud	Wolke	Nuage	Nube
amount	Bewolkungsgrad, Bedeckung	Quantité de nuages, Nébulosité	Quantità di nubi Nuvolosità
Depression (USA:cyclone)	Zyklone, Tiefdruckgebiet, Depression	Cyclone, Dépression	Ciclone, Depressione
Fog	Nebel	Brouillard	Nebbia
Front	Front	Front	Fronte
Humidity	Luftfeuchte, Feuchtigkeit	Humidité de l'air	Umidità dell'aria

English	German	French	Italian
Occlusion	Okklusion	Dépression occlus	Occlusione
Precipitation	Niederschlag	Précipitations	Precipitazioni
drizzle	Nieseln	Bruine	Pioviggina
			Pioggerella
rain	Regen	Pluie	Pioggia
snow	Schnee	Neige	Neve
Ridge of high pressure	Hochdruckkeil	Crête anti-cyclonique	Cresta di alta pressione
Storm	Sturm	Orage	Tempesta
Sunshine	Sonnenschein	Insolation	Insolazione
Temperature	Temperatur	Température	Temperatura
fall in	Temperaturabnahme	Abaissement de la température	Caduta della temperatura
inversion	Temperatur Inversion	Inversion de la température	Inversione di temperatura
rise in	Temperaturzunahme	Augmentation de la température	Aumento della temperatura
Visibility	Sicht	Visibilité	Visibilità
Weather	Wetter	Temps	Tempo
change in	Wetterwechsel	Changement du temps	Cambiamento del tempo
worsening	Wetterveischlech-terung	Aggravation du temps	Peggioramento del tempo
forecast	Wettervoshersage Wetterprognose	Prévision de temps	Previsoione del tempo
map	Wetterkarte	Carte météorologique	Carta del tempo
Wind	Wind	Vent	Vento
breeze	Abrieb	Brise	Vento moderato Brezza
direction	Windrichtung	Direction du vent	Direzione del vento
speed	Windgeschwindigkeit	Vitesse du vent	Velocità del vento

Sometimes a forecast may be gleaned from the radio, which is how Alaskan climbers get theirs. At any rate it's worth going to some trouble to elicit a forecast from one source or another. After that you can temper it with the evidence of your own eyes – eyes that will be growing daily more observant – so that, though eyes and forecast will never entirely amount to omniscience, you should at least be able to avoid the worst of the weather.

Rob Collister breaking new ground on the East Ridge of Deborah, Alaska.

Nearing the summit of Deborah, Alaska while behind 'alps o'er alps arise'.

*Starting the South Ridge of the Aiguille de Sialouze (AD) Dauphiné
Alps. This is a fine, airy ridge and the beginning of an exciting traverse.
The Glacier du Sélé can be seen behind the climbers, from its source at
the Col de Sélé to the terminal moraine.*

High on the South Ridge of the Aiguille de Sialouze — a place where good balance is clearly an asset!

The summit of the Barre des Ecrins with Mont Pelvoux beyond.

The Nunatak, Alaska.

The Chamonix Aiguilles don a winter coat. The left hand peak is the
Aiguille de Blaitière.

The Aiguille de Dru, and behind, wearing a plume of cloud, the
Aiguille Verte. The Verte holds a number of grand easy and middle
grade routes; the Dru a number of equally grand, but rather hard, rock
routes.

(Above) 'Bliss it was that dawn to be alive.' Looking east from the Col du Sélé at sunrise.

(Right) The author on steep alpine ice on a new route on the North Face of the Aiguille de Leschaux in the Mont Blanc massif.

*Pete Boardman grapples with a mile of ridge on Gauri Sankar, Nepal;
at 23,000 ft a larger than average alp.*

*Super lightweight alpinism at 17,000 ft on Raven's Pyramid in the
Karakoram; a 22 pitch rock route with difficulties up to 6a (British).
Climber: Mick Hardwick – Photo: Pat Littlejohn.*

A view through ice across Alaska from Mt. Hess.

CHANGES IN CONDITIONS BY THE TIME OF DAY

Alpine conditions vary enormously by the time of day. At night, it is usually sufficiently cold to freeze the snow that may have been softened by the day's sun, and to freeze to ice or verglas water that may have resulted from the sun's heat on snow or ice. It is this nightly freeze that produces the névé, the frozen snow surface, that we all hope for: it is stable, we may dance across the surface rather than sink in to our shins or deeper and it is a joy to climb on. So a clear night sky and consequent freeze are welcome, indeed essential.

But as the sun rises so does the temperature. The surface of the snow softens and then melts, and by midday you are in to your shins again.

In essence then, the effects of these daily variations in temperature are:
1. Frozen snow (névé) is stable, easy to walk over, good to climb on.
2. Snow that hasn't frozen the night before, or which has by mid-afternoon been softened by the sun is unstable and therefore avalanche-prone, feet sink into the snow and that is tiring, steps on snow slopes give way – tiring and insecure; and snow bridges over crevasses are weakest when soft and wet (*see* page 133).
3. Stonefall is most common on slopes that catch the sun, which then melts the ice or verglas that has been cementing those rocks overnight, triggering their release (*see* page 108).

Other factors affecting these general observations are:

1. *Altitude*: generally speaking the higher the colder (by approximately 3°C per 300m or 1000ft).
2. *Cloud Cover*: at night cloud acts as a blanket and stops the day's warmth from escaping. The snow's surface is unlikely to freeze during a cloud-covered night, and this may put paid to the next day's plans. Don't despair prematurely, however. A cloud-covered night may clear by the small hours leaving enough time for the snow to freeze before dawn – so that your chosen route may still be 'on'.
3. *Aspect*: a north face receives very little sun so that it will always be fairly cold. The daily variations in conditions will therefore not be marked. Note though, that few of the so-called north faces are strictly north-facing so that many a north face basks at some time of the day, early if it inclines to the east, late if to the west. East faces get sun in the morning before it is very hot – and in any case a cold day may result in refreezing before the day is done. Conversely, west faces get the sun late so they are cold in the morning, warm at evening. South-facing aspects get sun far longer than others and so they are the warmest.

Some parts of a face may be in shadow while another basks in sun. When this happens (particularly in couloirs, *see* page 158) sun on a higher part of the mountain may unleash a fusillade of stones on a lower part. Climbing in shadow does not necessarily mean climbing in safety: look above to see what will happen. Stonefall is often at its worst about an hour after the sun has struck the top of a face, which is what happens, rather too frequently on the North Face of the Eiger, perhaps the most notorious for sun-triggered stonefall.

And so, in deference to these diurnal changes in conditions, the alpine start was

97

born; that practice of begining an alpine day well before dawn – especially if the day involves much glacier or snow or ice work – so that as much of the ascent as possible is completed before the sun makes things too dangerous. On a big route this may mean leaving the hut as early as 1 a.m., and if, on shorter climbs, it means finishing before noon, then so much the better, the descent can be completed before the sun has softened and loosened the snow and perhaps before you have been overtaken by a change in the weather. And you'll have the latter part of the afternoon to sunbathe, enjoy the views, and rest and recuperate for more of the same on the morrow. In practice, on alpine routes of average length and moderate difficulty a climbing day will begin around 2–3 a.m., and finish by 11 a.m.–noon.

It is important to appreciate the effects of these daily changes. They seem obvious to me as I write this now but twenty years ago in New Zealand for my first alpine season they were far from obvious, as I recorded in *The Great Climbing Adventure* (Oxford Illustrated Press). In this case it was something of a misadventure:

'We couldn't work out what to do about the soft snow that sapped our energies in minutes. We tried making skis from bits of wood, snow shoes from cardboard, but nothing worked very well. Because the plateau was flat, featureless and apparently uncrevassed – camouflaged as it was by a thick blanket of snow – we didn't think to rope up to cross it and for three days we floundered around in blissful ignorance criscrossing heaven knows how many crevasses until, on the third day, Dave and I dropped into a crevasse together as we stood chatting. It was a providentially small slot, too narrow to fall into for more than a few feet. We scrambled out shaken. After that we roped up. But we still hadn't solved this soft snow business.

One night at about 1 a.m. Stu got up for a pee. It was a clear moonlit night and it drew him outside well beyond the normal tiptoe peeing spot by the door. There was a shout, "Yipee. That's it, by Christ, that's it," and he reappeared at the door in a state of wild excitement.

"Hey, fellas, come and see this, come on, come on."

Sleepily we shuffled out. The moonlit panorama was certainly stunning but Stu wasn't looking at the view, he was jumping up and down on the snow, then dropping to his knees and pummelling the frozen surface like a thing demented. The frozen surface!

"It's hard, it's hard, it's bone-bloody-hard!"

And we all joined in the dance, leaping about in our stocking feet. We had discovered the "alpine start".

Had we read anything at all about mountains we would have known, but we hadn't and didn't. Had there been anyone else in the hut we would have found out, but there wasn't. It seems hardly credible that we didn't know that since the dawn of alpinism men and women in their hundreds have been struggling from their slumbers at 2 and 3 in the morning and acting out that benighted purgatory known the mountain world over as the "alpine start". Now we knew. And what a difference it made.

An hour later, all girded and loined, we skittered across the glacier bettering all previous times to the foot of the route.'

Local Variations

If you are lucky enough to be able to spend some time in one alpine area, you'll begin to get acquainted with the idiosyncrasies of its weather. Storms in the Mont Blanc area for example tend to be foretold by a build-up of cloud on Mont Blanc itself and also perhaps on the Aiguille Verte – especially significant if the cloud is drifting in from the south. Weather forming on these summits will usually affect the general area, though often nowhere outside the general area, so that the peaks, of Arolla and of Zermatt, further east, might remain clear.

Bernese Oberland storms are notoriously sudden and often severe; those of the Dauphiné, an area blessed with better weather than most, can be equally sudden, though not usually as severe. Other areas such as the Bregalia or the Bernina have frequent storms but seldom dangerous ones (the Piz Badile North-East Face, being a potentially dangerous exception). In the Mont Blanc range the jagged, corniculate tops of the Aiguilles, the summits of the Grand Capucin, and the South Ridge of the Noire, are notorious for lightning; not good places to be in electrical storms (*see* page 108). Even in comparatively small Alpine regions the weather may vary from area to area.

Looking again at Europe: at Zermatt, for example, a storm will often be centred on the Matterhorn and the Dent d'Herens leaving the Ober Gabelhorn and other peaks on that side of the range unscathed.

Always solicit a weather forecast, even if it is from the hut guardian (who will have probably got his from the radio) and then climb with a weather eye open. These things and steadily accumulating experience will steer you a fair course through the storms of hills.

AVALANCHES

An avalanche is a quantity of snow (and often ice too) tumbling down a mountain-

Fig 83   A small powder avalanche.

side. They vary in size from a slough of snow that may only be powerful enough to unbalance a climber to a cataclysmic ton of snow, hundreds of feet high and wide, that can devastate entire villages and lay waste to whole valleys.

A party involved in an avalanche may be injured or killed by:

1.   Boulders or ice blocks contained in the avalanche's mass.
2.   A long fall, perhaps over a cliff or other big drop that may lie in the avalanche's path.
3.   Burial when the avalanche comes to rest – particularly in the case of a wet snow avalanche. Wet snow holds no air, is impossible to breathe through, and in any case, entombs by its weight.
4.   Suffocation by snow-laden air in the case of a powder dry avalanche.

Snow slides are much more common than full-scale avalanches on climbing routes, and those of a cataclysmic nature are rare and confined mainly to winter months. But even the smallest snow slide may be sufficient to dislodge a climber and are, therefore, to be avoided.

Like weather forecasting, the assessment of avalanche risk is an imprecise science. No one understands the phenomenon perfectly, and avalanche experts have themselves been victims.

A number of very good books have been written on the subject (*see* Further Reading list). I recommend a thorough scan of them. They are all very readable and you need not be a scientist to enjoy or understand them. Whether or not a slope will avalanche depends on a complicated sum of a number of interacting factors: temperature, surfaces, snow depth, wind, angle, gravity, past

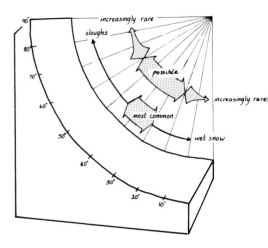

Fig 84   Likelihood of avalanche related to angle of slope.

weather, and probably a few more. You must at least recognise the fact that avalanches occur in alpine regions all year round – though they are more prevalent in spring when a winter's accumulation of snow is subjected to thaw conditions – and know in what circumstances they most readily happen, what types of avalanche are most common, and how to avoid them in the first place.

When?

In theory, an avalanche can happen on any slope above 18 degrees or so. More common angles, however, are between 30 degrees and 50 degrees. Above 50 degrees they are rare because snow seldom accumulates in sufficient depth on a slope of that steepness. Any snow slope or gully is potentially prone to avalanches. Dangerous times are:

1.   When it is snowing heavily (a rate of 1in (2.5cm) an hour is considered heavy in this context).

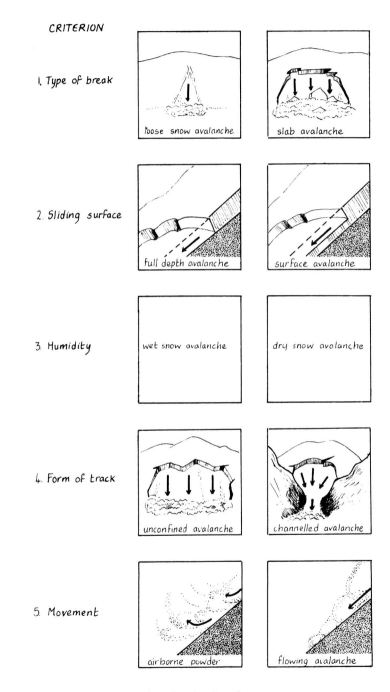

Fig 85   An internationally-recognised avalanche classification.

2.   Two or three days after it has snowed heavily.

3.   During thaws (wet snow slides and cornices falling).

4.   *Any period when wind and snow have co-incided* (including wind-driven, old snow).

Avalanche Types

For the mountaineer's purpose, there are two broad divisions of avalanches: loose and slab. A loose snow avalanche has little internal cohesion and moves in a formless mass, beginning at a single point, in wet or dry snow, and broadening as it gathers momentum. Loose dry snow moves more quickly but is less imprisoning than loose wet snow, which slides slowly but weighs heavily on a victim. The latter is the more common loose snow avalanche in Alpine summer seasons.

Slab avalanches occur when an area of windslab snow (that is, snow that has been compacted by the wind) breaks away in a

Fig 87   *Loose snow avalanches, each with a characteristic inverted fan slope. These avalanches have been deliberately triggered by controlled explosions, (the craters are clearly visible) as part of the avalanche safety control at a ski resort. The effect would have been much the same had nature had her way.*

Fig 86   *A mountaineer falls victim to a loose snow avalanche, and is held by his partner.*

Fig 88   Slab avalanche. In this case a full depth slab avalanche (see classification Fig 85), the sliding surface for which has been the area of relatively smooth black rock.

blanket, leaving a clearly defined fracture line. On the mountainside the climber is often both trigger and victim. The slab so released varies from yards to acres square, and is characterised by internal cohesion. Windslab is that snow deposited on the lee slope when wind and snow combine. That this can occur during snowfall will be obvious, but don't forget that snow, being a loose, mobile substance, can be blown about after it has ceased to snow. When this happens, it may be by a new wind from a different direction – beware.

It can be packed surprisingly hard (variations in the strength characteristics of snow are among the widest found in nature:

the hardness of wind-packed snow may be 50,000 times that of light powder snow). It can also be deceptively hard, giving the appearance and feel of névé. Be suspicious. It is betrayed by a matt surface and exploration with an axe will soon reveal its slab nature. Treat all lee slopes with circumspection, particularly after long periods of winds prevailing from a particular direction. As has already been explained, the area immediately beneath a cornice (a wind-formed feature) will often consist of wind-slabbed snow. Of the two broad types, slab avalanches are the more dangerous because they are less predictable and better disguised.

Fig 89   Two views of a small slab avalanche. (a) At first sight it looks like a loose snow avalanche, beginning as it does from a single point.

(b) Closer inspection, however, reveals the slab layers. What is interesting is the gentle angle on which this avalanche occurred – about 20°.

AVOIDING AVALANCHES

Reading Ground

Steep gullies (the line of the majority of winter routes) and open snow slopes are natural avalanche paths. Ridges, outcrops and terraces are natural avalanche barriers. Ridges are always the safest place in terrain prone to avalanches. If, for instance, it has been snowing heavily for two days and you are determined to bag a route, try to make it a ridge or a buttress. Better advice, though, is not to climb at all until the new snow has had time to settle – one or two days at least.

Rock outcrops are islands of safety. Rough, irregular ground tends to hold back slides, at least until the irregularities have been filled in and smoothed over with snow.

Smooth ground, or ground on which grass is lying flattened, offer good sliding slopes to just a few inches of snow.

The avalanche potential of a given slope usually recedes with time – until it snows again.

Safety Points

1.   Whenever practical, expose only one member of the team at a time. The other might well be belayed at the side of a gully or to a rock outcrop.
2.   Try to steer clear of the avalanche paths.
3.   Don't stop or rest under an avalanche path.
4.   Avoid times of greatest danger, that is, during or immediately after a snowfall of more than 1in (2.5cm) an hour, or after prolonged periods of high wind.

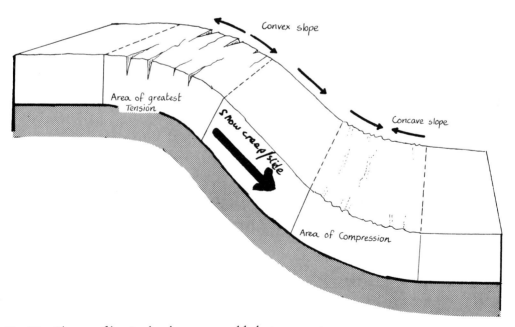

Fig 90   Slope profile. Avalanches are most likely to occur at convex areas where the tensions within the snow cover are greatest.

5.   Be aware of the temperature: the colder it is, the longer new snow remains dangerous. Common sense tells us, however, that new, wet snow followed by a severe frost will quickly produce stable, safe and superb climbing conditons.
6.   Beware lee areas and especially those below cornices.
7.   Keep to gully sides and walls.
8.   Cross potential avalanche slopes as high as possible, hugging the foot of any buttresses.
9.   If you must climb on an avalanche slope:
   (a) Close up your clothing, don hat and mitts and raise your hood (all of these actions increase your chances of survival if buried).
   (b) Loosen rucksack straps so that it can be jettisoned if necessary.
   (c) Climb directly up or down, rather than across, when possible.
   (d) You might consider trailing an avalanche cord from your belt. There is a chance that an inch or two of it will remain on the surface, even though you are buried.
   (e) Take advantage of any protection that nature has provided, such as rock outcrops or ridges.

Notes for Victims

If you are caught in an avalanche:

1.   Call out so that other members of your party can watch your course in case you are buried.
2.   Try to delay your departure. In a small slide you may be able to plant an axe and hang on long enough to avoid being swept away. Even if you are carried away, the longer you can delay, the less snow there will be to follow you and to bury you.

3.   Discard your rucksack.
4.   Attempt, with a swimming motion, to stay on the surface. Try to work to one side of the moving snow. In a large or fast-moving avalanche these efforts will probably be of little avail, but they may save your life in a smaller one.
5.   If you find these efforts are not helping, cover your face with your hands. This will help keep snow out of your nose and mouth, and you will have a chance to clear a breathing space if you are buried. Avalanche snow often becomes very hard as soon as it stops moving. You may not be able to move your arms once the snow has stopped.
6.   If you are buried, try not to panic. Frantic and fruitless efforts to free yourself consume valuable oxygen. Stern self-control is essential to survival.
7.   In soft snow you may be able to dig yourself out, or at least make room to breathe. Make sure you dig upwards, towards the surface. Avalanche victims sometimes lose their sense of direction and try to dig down.
8.   If you hear rescuers working above you, don't waste your strength by shouting. Though sound transmits into snow easily, it transmits out poorly.

Notes for Survivors

1.   Don't panic – the lives of your buried mates may depend on what you do in the next hour. Check for further slide danger and pick a safe escape route in case of a repeat avalanche.
2.   Mark the last point where victims were seen on the avalanche path. This will narrow the area of your search and that of the rescue party. Use an ice axe, rucksack, rope, or clothing as a marker.
3.   Make a quick search. If there are only

two or three survivors, they must make a quick but careful search of the avalanche area before going for help. If at all possible, one survivor should be left to continue the search and guide the rescue party.

4. Search the surface below the last point where the victim was seen for evidence of him or clues to his whereabouts. Mark the position of any pieces of equipment you may find – these will provide clues as to the victim's path. Search carefully and kick up the snow to uncover anything which may lie just beneath the surface.

5. If you are the sole survivor, you must still make a thorough search of the avalanche before going for help. This may seem obvious, but it is a rule all too often neglected. Even the simplest search may enable you to find the victim and free him alive.

6. If a rescue party can be summoned only after several hours or longer, the survivors must concentrate on making as thorough a search as possible with their own resources. The chances of a buried victim being recovered alive diminish rapidly after two hours.

7. If the initial search fails, begin probing with your axe. Trees, ledges, benches or other terrain features which have caught the snow are the most likely places. If there are several survivors, probing at likely spots can continue until a rescue party arrives. If you are alone, you will have to decide when to break off the search and seek help.

8. Send for help. If there are several survivors, send only two. The remaining survivors must search for the victim in the meantime. If it will take two hours or more for help to reach the scene, and the avalanche is not too large, the victim may have a better chance if everyone remains to search. This is a difficult decision to make,

and depends on circumstances.

9. The rescue party will normally expect you to guide them back to the accident scene unless its location is absolutely clear.

10. If the victim is found, treat him immediately for suffocation and shock. Free his nose and mouth of snow and administer mouth-to-mouth resuscitation if necessary. Clean snow from the inside of his clothing and place him in a sleeping bag, with his head downhill. The very gentle application of external heat will help counteract severe chilling. Any further injuries should then be treated according to standard first-aid practices.

A summary of action to take is:

1. Check for further danger.
2. Mark last point seen.
3. Quick search.
4. Thorough search.
5. Send for help.

Serac or Cornice Collapse

Avalanches are sometimes triggered by the collapse of a serac (*see* page 117) or cornice (*see* 159). The resultant avalanche may consist solely of the broken debris of that serac or cornice, or of the debris mixed with a mass of snow on which the collapse has fallen: collapsing seracs and cornices are devastatingly effective triggers of avalanches. Immense amounts of ice are likely to be involved in the collapse of a serac which, moving with speed and weight, will have a profound effect on whatever lies in its path – and climbers especially. Seracs and cornices are unpredictable and may crash at any time of the day or night, although the most dangerous period is early afternoon when the sun is highest and hottest –

melting is a factor in collapse. Since they are pretty unpredictable the only practical precaution is to avoid them altogether; avoid standing on or below them. If this is not always possible (which, in truth, it isn't) then reduce your exposure to as short a time as you can, by moving quickly across their path or off their line.

STONEFALL

Stonefall is common in alpine areas. It may arise from the dislodgement of already loose rock – and rock is often climbed in the alps (for example, in the Pennine Alps of Europe, or on Mt. Cook of the Southern Alps) that would be left well alone by any self-respecting cragrat. Or it may be caused by the thaw/freeze action of snow and water: snow melts by day to water which seeps into cracks; water freezes by night and in freezing expands, breaking away a chunk of rock along the line of the crack but holding it in ice until the sun warms it the next day: then stonefall (*see* Fig 155). So the sun is the enemy here: no sun, no stonefall.

Stones may also be dislodged by climbing parties above. If you're lucky the falling stones will be preceded by a cry of '*attention pierres*' or the Italian or German equivalent. (You don't have to be trilingual, the cry itself is the warning.) If you dislodge stones yourself and you know or think that there might be others beneath shout 'below' – again it is the sound that is the warning, not the translation. Some places are notorious for stonefall and the guidebook will probably make mention of them. Faces, couloirs and gullies are the most dangerous places; ridges, arêtes and butteresses, the least. Time of day and aspect are both factors affecting the frequency and severity of stonefall (*see* pages 97 and 88).

Falling stones quickly gather speed (and no moss) and before long are whirring bullet-like through the air. They soon accumulate enormous energy, all of which is visited on the hapless mountaineer should he be struck by the missile. The sooner you take cover the better, cower under overhangs, lie flat in the shadow of bulging rocks, or shrink under your helmet – that's the first reason you're wearing it.

LIGHTNING

The standard text on lightning is to be found in Eric Langmuir's excellent handbook, '*Mountaincraft and Leadership*', published jointly by the Scottish Sports Council and the Mountain Walking Leader Training Board (second edition 1984), and is reproduced here by kind permission of the Scottish Sports Council.

'Lightning can hardly be regarded as a major mountain hazard yet every year it claims the lives of two or three mountaineers. Like the winter avalanche it is commonly regarded as an Act of God and the very impartiality with which it chooses its victims encourages a fatalistic outlook among climbers and walkers. The actual physical process is now fairly well understood and this emphasises that there are certain simple precautions which can be taken to avoid a strike.

'The first thing to realise is that to be "struck" by lightning is by no means always fatal. True, a direct hit is likely to be so, but more often than not the victim receives only a part of the stroke, either by induction, because he happens to be standing near, or through the ground in the form of earth currents which dissipate, like the roots of a tree, from the source. Such partial shocks need not be fatal though they could, of course, cause death indirectly if the climber should fall off or be rendered incapable of fending for himself. The stroke itself is a variable quantity, being the product of a very large current (thousands of amps) and a very short time (thousandths of a second). In many cases a much smaller current in contact for a few seconds could cause considerably more damage. Fortunately, there is usually some advance warning of the approach of an electrical storm and avoiding action can be taken, but once in the firing line decisions tend to be taken out of your hands. Anyone who has experienced the literally hair-raising preliminaries will vouch for this. Ice axes hum and spark, the skin tingles and local projections glow with a bluish light.

'Lightning is usually associated with the towering cumulonimbus type of cloud which heralds the passing of a cold front. The occasional flash followed by a roll of thunder should be warning enough that an electrical storm is on its way. The sound will travel at a speed of 1km per 3 seconds, so by timing the interval between the flash and the thunder you can estimate your distance from the storm.

'During a storm, strikes tend to be concentrated on mountain tops or other natural projections from the general surroundings. At the same time, since such points "service" a fairly wide area, there tends to be a shaded or relatively safe zone associated with them. The peak must be at least 7m high and the relatively safe zone is of the same order horizontally. Note that it affords no protection to be tucked in against the cliff or peak itself since in this position you are likely to receive earth currents shed from the peak.

'The natural inclination in a really violent storm is to seek shelter, especially if rain is driving down. Unfortunately, this is quite the wrong thing to do unless you can find a cave which gives you at least 3m head room and 1m on either side. Such caves and hollows in the rock are often simply local expansions of natural fissures. These in turn are the likely conduits for earth currents, especially if they hold water and by sheltering in them you are offering yourself as a convenient alternative to the spark gap.

'Exactly the same argument applies to sheltering under large boulders. With reasonably waterproof clothing, remaining dry should not be a major problem and it is much safer to sit it out in the open. Try to find a broken scree slope, preferably in a safe zone and sit on top of a dry rope or rucksack with your knees up and your hands in your lap. Do not attempt to support yourself on your hands or by leaning back. The object of these precautions is to keep your points of contact with the ground as close together as possible and in such a position that a current flowing along the ground would tend to pass through a non-vital part of the body.

'On a cliff face, sit out the storm on the nearest ledge, but avoid chimneys and fissures of any kind. If a belay is necessary, try to avoid using the wet rope as a natural lead from a vertical crack to your body. On an exposed peak or ridge your position is much more serious and it is normally advisable to make some attempt to get at least part way down even at the height of the storm. Abseiling in an electrical storm is a risky manoeuvre, but it is normally preferable to a position on the lightning highway of an exposed ridge. In any event, one or two rope lengths may well take you to a position of relative safety. If you do abseil, use a dry rope if you have the choice and use a safety

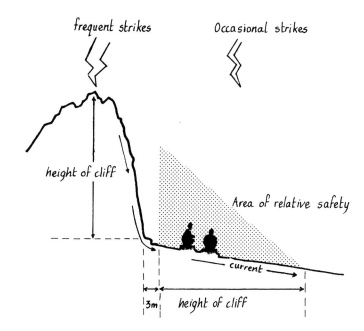

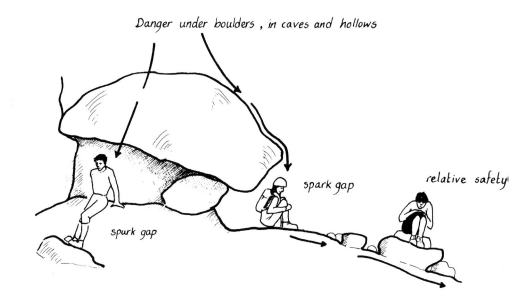

Fig 91   *Sheltering from lightning.*

rope. Fatal accidents have often resulted from a non-fatal strike which in the first instance, has merely stunned the victim.

'It is fashionable, too, to discard pieces of extraneous equipment; cameras, rucksacks, crampons and even ice-axes, under the mistaken impression that they "attract" lightning. They don't, any more than you do yourself. The electrical resistance of the average wooden-shafted axe between head and spike is almost five times that of the human body. If it is humming and sparking it may be prudent to lay it down carefully beside you but no more. The axe is too valuable a tool to be tossed away in a storm. It may well be needed to deal with icy rocks on the retreat.'

There's nothing to add to that except to emphasise the importance of taking evasive action – which may be up or down or across – at the first warning, especially if you are on a notoriously lightning-prone mountain like the Grand Capucin of Mont Blanc. An electric storm that sizzled and sparked around Dave Nicholls and I, trapped on the summit of that dramatic peak, still notes as one of my more nightmarish mountain experiences. A more careful scan of the weather forecast might have spared us the ordeal but we were young then and took little heed of such, as we thought, counsels of timidity. We nearly fried for our arrogance and now assiduously note the weatherman's helpful detail – though forecasting is as yet an imprecise science and not all electrical storms, still less all lightning strikes, are foreseen.

GLACIERS

Glaciers are rivers of ice which, fed by centuries of snow at and beyond their source, flow from upper snow-fields to

Fig 92   The Tasman Glacier, a river of ice 20 miles long.

Fig 93   *Les Bans in the Dauphiné: acres of rough red rock guarded by glacier.*

Fig 94   *The Pilatte Glacier below Les Bans in the Dauphiné.*

lower valleys. They vary greatly in length and steepness and complexity. The longest in the European Alps is the Aletsh Glacier in the Bernese Oberland, at 22 miles long and over 1,000ft thick. The Tasman Glacier of the Southern Alps of New Zealand is 20 miles long, the mighty Baltoro in the Karakoram nearly 50 – and still by no means the longest glacier in the world.

Glaciers and references thereto are always viewed looking in the direction of flow – as with a river – unless otherwise specified. So that the left bank, for example, will actually be on your right hand if you are walking *up* the glacier. This is not as confusing as it may at first appear and most

guidebooks are scrupulously careful in avoiding misunderstandings.

Glacier Features and Nomenclature

(The alphabetical references correspond to the same features on the photograph.)

Dry Glacier (A)

By mid-season many glaciers are dry in their lower regions. This means that the snow cover has melted or evaporated, exposing the bare ice of the glacier underneath. Dry glaciers are rather ugly but usually safe for

Fig 95   The névé of the Barre des Ecrins, source of the Glacier Blanc.

Fig 96   High above the Glacier Blanc, Massif des Ecrins. Note the patterns of crevasses. This was late August and the glacier, which is usually amply covered in snow, is now nearly dry – hence all those open crevasses.

travel because the crevasses are readily espied and easily avoided. It is often safe to cross dry glaciers unroped – though beware the odd still hidden crevasse covered with a stubborn camouflage of snow – tiger trap-like. Glaciers that are dry in their lower reaches are still usually snow-covered in their middle and upper reaches, where crevasses may be partly or wholly concealed and where the rope should most certainly be deployed.

In fact the word 'dry' is something of a misnomer since many so-called glaciers are ankle deep in melt-water by mid afternoon. Snow-less would be a more accurate description, but 'dry' it is, no matter how wet.

Hanging Glacier (B)

This is a glacier on a steep face – there is no precise angle at which a glacier graduates to hanging status: it is mainly a question of appearance. Glaciers that fall over rock faces are also described as hanging glaciers. These tend to be rapidly moving, sending down frequent ice avalanches whenever gravity wins the pull.

Crevasses (C)

These are cracks or splits in the glacier ice, caused by stresses of compression, and stretching. Crevasses range in depth from a few feet to a few hundred feet, and in width

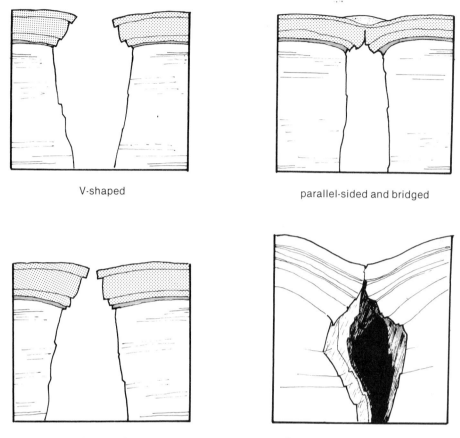

V-shaped

parallel-sided and bridged

A-shaped

diamond-shaped and bridged

*Fig 97   Crevasses are often more than they seem: 4 typical cross-sections.
The crevasses with A and diamond cross-sections will always be the hardest
to escape from because the victim is likely to be hanging in space. In either
of the other two you stand a good chance of being able to use at least the
feet, and probably the hands too, to assist evacuation.*

from an easy step to impassable gulfs. In winter and more rarely, in the summer, even the largest of crevasses may be covered by snow bridges – though this is not necessarily an advantage, for although a good bridge will afford you passage, a weak bridge may break and land you and partner with a problem, not to mention the crevasse.

The British have borrowed much of their glacier terminology from the French – though not exclusively. A *moulin*, for example, is a stream that disappears into a crevasse, and *Névé* (Fig 95) is a snow-field that feeds a glacier and by association hard-packed snow.

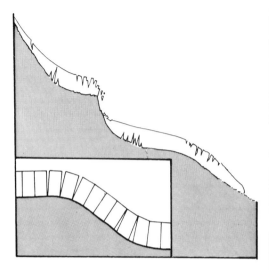

Fig 98   Profiles through a glacier on
varying angles of terrain. A gentle dip
(lower profile) causes crevasses to open: a
sudden step (top profile) produces an ice fall.

Fig 99   Looking down 2,000ft at a pattern
of crevasses on the Glacier Noir, Dauphiné.

Fig 100   A party pauses by a sizeable crevasse during the descent of the
Violettes Glacier which flows off Mount Pelvoux in the Dauphiné.

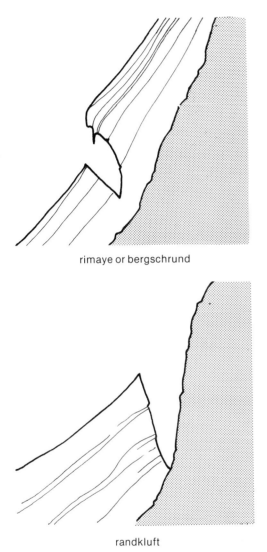

rimaye or bergschrund

randkluft

*Fig 101   Top: rimaye or bergschrund;
bottom: randkluft.*

Rimaye (E)

This is that usually large crevasse where the glacier parts company with the mountain. We also, perhaps in fact more frequently, call this feature a *bergschrund* (from German). (Strictly speaking the crevasse that separates

a glacier from the rock of a mountain, as opposed to separating snow from snow, is a *randkluft*, but most of us continue to call them all rimayes or bergschrunds, the latter shortened to a neat 'schrund' by most Americans.) There are sometimes multiple bergschrunds all with the upper lip characteristically higher than the lower. Such a phenomenon can present an insuperable obstacle, especially in ascent. In descent they may still prove serious (*see* page 132). These things are especially true late in the season when bergschrunds are at their widest and barest.

Serac (F)

A serac is a wall, tower or pinnacle of glacier ice. They are often unstable and their collapse is a common avalanche trigger (*see* page 107). Nor may their collapse, caused by the movement of the glacier's ice, be predicted – though it is slightly more likely to happen in the heat of the day, than in the cool of the night.

Icefall (G)

A steep section of glacier with convoluted crevasses and contorted seracs – often in a state of near or total collapse. Short, not so steep icefalls may be passed in reasonable security; those of steeper longer falls are best circumnavigated.

Moraines (H)

These are formed by the boulders and rubble bulldozed by a glacier and carried down on its back or pushed before its snout. Some moraines are hundreds of feet high.

Terminal moraine forms at the snout of a glacier – or further down the valley if the

Fig 102 An icefall underneath the Jungfrau, Bernese Oberland.

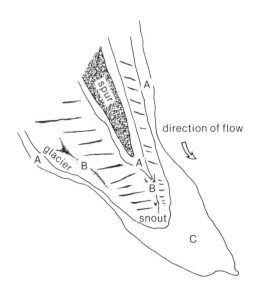

Fig 103 Three kinds of moraine: lateral (A); medial (B); terminal or end (C).

glacier is retreating, as most of them are. *Lateral moraines* form along the banks of the glacier and *medial moraines* are long moraines in the middle of glaciers, usually the result of the conjuction of two glaciers uniting two lateral moraines.

The sides of moraines are often loose and tiring to walk or climb on though good paths frequently run along their crests where the passage of time and thousands of feet have made a firm path by which difficult sections of glacier can be avoided. However, beware moraines in heavy rain when they are prone to subsidence.

Not all moraines are what they appear: some may be little more than a sprinkling of earth and boulders concealing large crevasses. However, whenever a moraine bears a clear path it is likely to be the best way.

Fig 104   A moraine path on the approach to the Triolet Glacier.

Snout (I)

This is the bottom end of the glacier and often an area of enormous crevasses. A river, and a cold one, usually issues from below a snout.

GLACIER TRAVEL

Most alpine routes involve some glacier work and even when those routes are entirely rock – and rock which you have elected to climb in lightweight rock boots – there may still be a glacier or snow-covered approach. An interesting exception is the North Face of the Eiger which is approached across green meadows dotted with buttercups, edelweiss and cows, but then the way down leads to a glacier, so the general rule holds good. More usually, even of the easiest of alpine climbs, it will be necessary to cross or ascend a glacier to reach the start of the route – whether it be rock, or ice or mixed – and then to negotiate the same glacier at the end of the day when returning to the hut or another glacier if descending to a place other than that morning's start point. Many classic alpine routes involve hours of travel on glaciers. And these glaciers make certain procedures necessary – vital even.

ROPING UP

Dry glaciers, that is glaciers where the ice is bare of snow and all the crevasses are clear to see, can often be safely traversed unroped. On all snow-covered, or even half-covered, glaciers, it is prudent to rope up, no matter how well trodden the path, or how easy the way. Crevasses are no respecters of climbers and may open beneath the best; or a snow bridge may fail unexpectedly. Roping up is not an onerous task and with only a little practice takes but a few minutes. Indeed, overall, it may save time since, once roped, you'll be able to move faster and with greater freedom than if you were tentatively probing your way round unroped. There are half a dozen practicable ways of roping up but those described here work as well as any.

Since most alpine climbs are conducted in teams of two then it is that number that I will concentrate on. It is not, however, the safest number for glacier travel, three being safer and four safer still. With numbers greater than that on one rope there is little to worry about – beyond confusion. If one of the team falls into a crevasse he can easily

119

be pulled out by the others, rather like a cork from a champagne bottle if the number pulling is great enough. There are various opinions about who should go first and who should bring up the rear – and there may be differing opinions once actually on the glacier too! If there is a more experienced climber on the rope it makes some sense for him *not* to go first – he can play a more useful role from the surface than from the depths of a crevasse and it is usually the first on the rope who falls in if anyone is going to, though not always. Similarly, if one climber is significantly lighter than the remainder then he might volunteer to go ahead – or he might not! It is a reasonable thing though, especially going downhill when a heavy climber will hold a lighter one more easily than the other way around.

Method for Roping Up

Climbers should be spaced along the rope about 30ft (9m) apart. (This distance may have to be greater if there are especially wide crevasses about.) Two climbers on either end of a 45m rope can best place themselves 9m apart by shortening the rope as shown. Middlemen tie in at 9m intervals (having allowed for coils as shown in Figs 105 to 113).

Taking Coils

There is some argument about whether these coils should be taken under or over the rucksack straps. In essence: do you take coils and then shoulder your sack, or the other way around? As with most things in mountaineering there are pros and cons, which are, if coils are placed under the straps:

1. Pro: The rucksack may be removed (for

whatever reason) without first lifting off the coils. This may be particularly relevant when you are dangling in a crevasse and keen to get the weight of that sack from your back and directly on to the rope (*see* Fig 137). It's not easy if coils are over straps.
2. Cons:
    (a) The arrangement may prove uncomfortable especially if a heavy sack is carried.
    (b) You have to remove the sack to take the coils in the first place – and every time after that when you need to release coils.

The counter-argument merely reverses these points. On balance the argument seems to favour coils over; but there is no right and wrong.

Even if you intend to climb on a double rope later in the day, it is as well to rope up with a single rope for glacier travel, leaving the second stowed in a rucksack. Encountering a glacier after a climb, remove one rope.

Both members of the team will now be carrying around their torsos about 15–18m of rope (about 12 coils). When coiled and tied off in the manner shown this is not uncomfortable or cumbersome.

It is not uncommon to see a team of climbers roped in this (or a similar way) for negotiating glaciers but in addition, one or more or all the party are carrying coils of rope in a hand. This is a mistake. Coils to hand make good sense when moving together on the mountain (*see* page 150) but no sense at all when moving together over a glacier – and it is the glacier that makes the distinction. All that the carrying of hand coils on a glacier means is that whoever is unlucky enough to fall into a crevasse will fall further by the combined length of the hand coils held by himself and his immediate

Fig 105   Take 12–14 coils around the body and over one shoulder. These should be fairly snug under the arm, though not so snug that they constrict or are uncomfortable.

Fig 106   A better, more convenient assembly results if the coils are taken under the arm and over the shoulder, than is the case the other way round.

Fig 107   When you judge that you have taken sufficient rope – 12–14 coils are normal on a rope of two (unless you are Brobdingnagian or Lilliputian!) reach under the coils and pull through a bight of the live rope – that is the rope running to your partner.

Fig 108   The length of this bight is important: the measure is that before the knot is tied it should reach to just below the waist belt.

(a)   (b)

Fig 109   (a) and (b): Using the bight, tie a figure of eight knot (see
Appendix III) embracing the live rope.

Fig 110   Judge things so that the resultant
loop, which should be as small as possible,
just reaches the waist tie-in point.

partner. The theory, propounded in support
of this practice, that coils give both faller and
fall-holder more time to react is nonsense –
as anyone who has fallen fifteen feet further
into a crevasse than was necessary will surely
agree. So, the rope between all members of
the party should be kept as tight as practical.
This takes constant vigilance and frequent
change of individual pace.

It is a good practice to attach two prusik
loops to the climbing rope, close to the
rope's point of attachment to the harness.
One of these loops is a 'leg' loop, the other
for attachment to your harness should you
go down a crevasse. The spare of the 'leg'
loop can be stuffed into a pocket or waist
from where it can be easily withdrawn in
the event of a fall, which once held, and
with two loops to prusik on, will enable the
victim to extricate himself fairly readily. It is
worth practising prusiking and indeed all of

122

Fig 111   Attach that figure of eight knot to the tie-in loop or to the knot by which you are attached to the harness with a screwgate karabiner. Note: There are a number of ways in which a climbing rope is attached to a harness (and climber). If this has been achieved by karabiner in the first place then all you have to do is clip the bight from your coils into the same karabiner. If, however, and this is the case with both the harnesses shown here, the climbing rope is joined to the harness by tying directly into that harness, there will be no karabiner in situ. In this case the bight from the coils and the tie-in knot or tie-in loop will need a karabiner to link them.

Fig 112   Link harness and chest loops with a karabiner. Shortening the rope in this way also produces a most effective body harness, the more comfortable to hang in should you fall victim to a crevasse. In this case the body-harness effect would have been better still had the coils been a fraction more snug and the bight from the chest coils slightly shorter. (But our model survived.)

Fig 113   The same system shown on a different model of harness. Here the bight from the chest coils has been linked by karabiner to the harness tie-in loop, rather than to the tie-in knot. It matters, dare I say it, not.

Fig 114   Tying in middlemen. For glacier travel and moving together middlemen can be tied-in by a number of methods. The one shown here is as simple and effective as any: two figure of eight knots. When tying into the rope between two climbers in this way you should judge things so that when you have tied-in and taken coils (to shorten the rope and to give yourself a body harness on the glacier) you are about 30ft (9m) from the climbers on either side.

the procedure for crevasse escape at home beneath a bough or bridge or similar.

The rope from the first man will run immediately to his rear and he should have no need to hold it if the climber behind is doing his job in keeping it snugly taut. The second on the rope can use the shorter of the two prusik loops as a convenient handle. This gives him some control over the lie of

the rope while the party is on the move as well as something extra to hang on to, to help reduce the shock force of his partner's fall – if one occurs.

(a)

(b)

*Fig 115 (a) and (b)   Managing the rope with vigilance not constant enough!
The first climber is stopping to watch his mate across the snow bridge that he
himself has just safetly negotiated. The second man, however, would have
been wise to wait until all was ready before beginning his crossing. Moreover,
there's not much the first could hope to achieve from this standing position. A
sitting belay is the answer. And they're tied too closely in the first place. (I am
able to be wise about all this because I was that first man!)*

Fig 116   Attaching a handle loop — in this case with a Klemheist, a friction knot used as an alternative to the prusik.

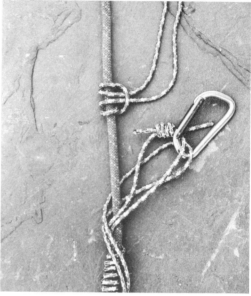

Fig 117   Prusik knot, and autoblock (top) (see also Appendix III).

Fig 118   Two prusik loops attached, one to be employed as a handle, the other tucked away into the harness.

Fig 119   Something to hang on to if a partner falls into a crevasse.

ROPE MANAGEMENT

As I have said, it is important to keep an eye on the rope: it should never be allowed to go slack between two climbers because, in the event of a fall, this would both greatly increase the difficulty of holding that fall and subject the victim to a longer fall than necessary. Apart from the discomfort, this both increases the chance of injury to the victim and adds to his difficulty in climbing out, for even if uninjured he will have further to go.

Managing the rope on the move takes some practice and even then it requires vigilance. When tired, perhaps at the end of a long day, it is all too easy to allow the rope to sag into the track where it will trip and ensnare and eventually infuriate the person in front. I have known teams of best mates fall into violence over such an apparently trivial matter. The moral is, the climber behind is responsible for the rope before; look well to it – especially at the end of a hard day when everyone is tired. The short prusik, attached as a handle, makes it easier to keep the rope from a fellow's feet.

Note: Having stated that you should rope up about 30ft (9m) apart, it is only fair to point out that some experienced alpinists prefer to travel much farther apart than that, and there are a few who argue that with only two on a rope then the farther apart the better. Whatever space you elect to put between, remember it is important to have enough rope spare in coils (or in a rucksack) to use in rescuing the victim from the crevasse. Adherents to the 'as far apart as possible' school will sometimes tie on to either end of a 45m rope and travel that far apart, but only if they have a spare rope – say a second 9mm – handy. On the whole, around 30ft (9m) seems the best compromise.

THE EFFECT OF CONDITIONS

The variations in conditions, already described (*see* page 88) affect glaciers as much as anything. Snow-covered glaciers are at their safest early in the season when there will be ample snow cover, filling crevasses and bridging them with thick, strong spans.

As the season runs its course the summer sun will daily lick at that snow cover, thinning it, widening crevasses and weakening bridges. The time of day makes a difference too. Early in the morning after a night's frost and before the arrival of the sun, or late in the afternoon when it has gone, the snow will be frozen; walking will be easier and safer, and bridges (and snow belays) will be stronger and safer.

In the middle part of the day, however, glaciers are hot places; and snow heavy and soft, and bridges at their weakest. Seracs are less stable too, at these times, a factor that should be taken into account in the overall plan for a day. Whenever possible, cross areas threatened by falling seracs as early or as late as possible. Where it is impossible to avoid such a danger, or where such avoidance would mean sitting idly for hours until dusk (such as on the Violettes Glacier descent from the Pelvoux, *see* Fig 100) then cross the threatened area at the greatest speed consistent with party safety: and I have seen some pretty wild sprints that were deemed to be consistent with party safety.

Fig 120   A biggish late-summer crevasse and a diminishing snow bridge, though probably still substantial enough to bear a climber's weight – perhaps at the crawl. Note the overhanging nature of the lip of the crevasse.

MOVEMENT ON GLACIERS

Glaciers vary in order of difficulty. Some are straightforward and a properly roped party will negotiate them with little more trouble than they'd have walking roped in the same fashion down a high street. Such glaciers are usually flattish, uniform and unconstricted with few underlying irregularities, changes in angle or compressions to disrupt their smooth flow. Seasonal and daily changes are still factors, but not significant. Other glaciers can be so difficult as to warrant being graded as a climb – the Glacier Long on the Ailefroide, for example, is graded Difficile. Still others, benign one year, may

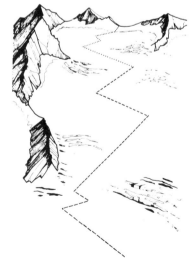

Fig 121   Choosing a line: avoidance of obstacles and danger is better than a cure.

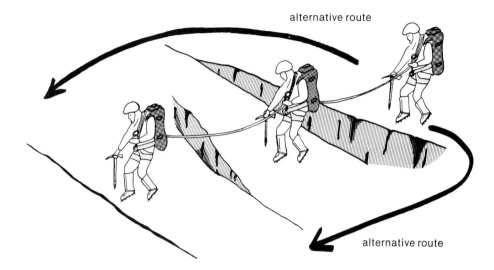

*Fig 122   Positioning. Single file is normal. Where crevasses are too wide
to step over, pick a route around.*

*Fig 123   Positioning. Sometimes it is impossible to avoid travelling in the
same direction as the run of the crevasses. If you are concerned that you
may all be aligned over the same crevasses you can stagger your formation
as shown − though it is seldom necessary.*

be ferocious the next – though this is rare. An example, however, is the glacier of the Clotte de L'homme, across whose snout climbers could scamper with impunity in 1979 only to find, that on their return the following season, it had advanced fully 100m and was now a sea of tumbling seracs and well nigh impassable – until a detour was contrived.

Unless you are the first party of the season on a particular glacier, or the first party after a heavy fall of snow, you are likely to have at least one set of tracks suggesting where the best route lies. A well used glacier will bear a positive trough, sometimes feet deep, where dozens of teams have trod a way. Existing tracks are very useful and often follow the safest and easiest line; *but not always and not necessarily*. It's worth considering what factors might be borne in mind when selecting a route up or down an untrodden glacier.

The two main factors governing your selections of route will be:

1. Avoidance of objective dangers – falling ice from seracs and icefalls, and falling rocks from overlooking spurs or buttresses.
2. Minimising crevasse difficulties – in this respect there are a number of other points to think about:
   (a) The middle of a glacier is usually the easiest.
   (b) At bends the outer bank will often be more badly crevassed than the inner.
   (c) Avoid ice-falls where possible.
   (d) Concealed crevasses are sometimes betrayed by a tell-tale dip in the snow's surface. Beware, probe with your axe and look to see if there isn't a better way.

Be aware of the direction of the crevasses. In an area where they are well concealed it is possible for an entire rope to be inadvertently travelling above the same crevasse. This can be avoided – although it is seldom necessary – by appropriate positioning within the party.

The aim is to be at right angles to the general direction of the crevasses. This usually happens more or less automatically since most crevasses are transverse and your direction of travel is mostly up or down a glacier. Sometimes, though, it is necessary to cross a glacier and it is on these occasions that you might find yourselves travelling in the same direction as the general lie of crevasses.

CROSSING CREVASSES

Detouring

The safest, though the slowest, way is not to cross them but to detour. This may result in a tortuous path. Detours will, however, be unavoidable where crevasses are too wide to be crossed by normal means. When you are unsure of your ground watch the rope, try to arrange things so that at least one member of the party is on terra firma, and rather than stand idly by while one member flounders or probes or searches, take up a belay so that he is protected.

Jumping

Sometimes the best way through is by jumping over a crevasse. Depending on the circumstances this may be preferred to a lengthy detour. It may, in cases where no detour exists, be the only solution. Choose the narrowest point of the crevasse and

Fig 124   *Nigel Shepherd, downhill and with the wind behind him, going for gold.*

Fig 125   *Jumping a crevasse: the belayer could have made herself progressively more secure by: (i) taking a body belay whilst still standing; (ii) sitting with a body belay; (iii) belaying conventionally to an anchor such as an ice-axe, deadman or buried rucksack.*

Fig 126   A team negotiates a small rimaye (bergschrund).

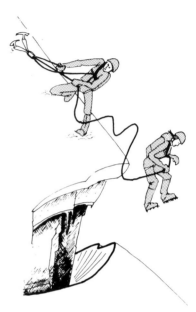

Fig 127   A team jumps a bergschrund (rimaye). The first jumps whilst the second belays . . .

ensure that your take-off 'pad' is secure, that it belongs to terra firma and not to something less permanent. In so far as you are able, check the landing site too. Nor is this any time for delusions of Olympian long jump prowess, though when you have looked and leapt, go for gold.

Take a few coils in your hand first, and discard them as you leap, so that you have enough slack rope to reach the other side. Don't jump without warning the rest of the party – unless it's an emergency – and it's better not to jump without the preparation outlined above. For big jumps get your partner to belay you and then jump, discarding coils in hand as you fly. Keep your feet well apart so that one does not spike the other on landing, and roll over beyond the landing point and away from the edge of the crevasse.

Clearly, downhill jumps are easier than uphill jumps. Exciting downhill jumps are

sometimes necessary on quite steep terrain – as when crossing a bergshrund (rimaye) in descent for example. Then not only should a belay be taken for the leader, but one should be considered for those following too. The procedure might look like that shown in Figs 127–129.

Greater belaying security can be achieved by fashioning an ice or snow bollard, and if the height loss is too great to contemplate a jump then the bollard can be used to abseil from (*see* Fig 173).

A bollard can be strengthened by placing ice-axes at the back between the rope and the snow or by packing it round with clothing or a rucksack before positioning the rope. Before departing the last man recovers it all – or if he is unsure of the integrity of the bollard and his pocket is bigger than his nerve, he may elect to

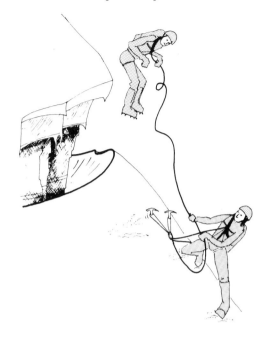

Fig 128 ... The axes are lowered (unnecessary if both climbers carry two) so that the first may belay while the second prepares to jump ...

Fig 129 ... The team is re-united. The second should be careful to avoid his mate – as both will assuredly agree! (Note: If the surface is hardened névé or ice, it might be better to abseil over such a bergschrund from an icescrew – if you are prepared to risk losing it – or from a bollard, as shown in Fig 173.)

abandon something of his clothing in the interests of safety. Alternatively, he may elect to abandon some of his mate's clothing. On such delicate social contracts are alpine partnerships forged or broken!

In ascent, bergschrunds should be tackled at their lowest point. Even then some climbing and a struggle is sometimes necessary.

CROSSING SNOW BRIDGES

Again, select the narrowest part of the crevasse and the stoutest-looking bit of snow bridge. Some snow bridges would bear a bus, others not the lightest-tripping

dancer. As already noted, bridges are at their best early in the season, or early in the morning or late at night; at their worst mid-morning to mid-afternoon. Prod with an axe where you are about to step to check that all is firm. If in doubt, distribute your weight more widely by crawling on hands and knees, or even on your stomach if necessary. The remainder of the party should take a belay, even if it is only sitting and niched deep into soft afternoon snow. Belay well back from the edge and keep the leader's rope snug between you. He'll not thank you from the middle of a tenuous bridge, mind wonderfully concentrated, for

133

Fig 130 Crossing a snow bridge. In this case the bridge is a substantial one; nevertheless the rope is good and tight to a belaying partner.

Fig 131 Crossing a snow bridge: if it is at all suspect and if you must cross, then distribute your weight over as great an area as possible – that is, crawl.

any slack. The leader, once across, may then belay the rest of the team if necessary.

If you feel yourself breaking through into a crevasse try to lunge forwards or backwards to the nearest bank. Spread arms and legs wide to blunt your penetration so that even if you fail to make either bank you may at least stick where you are, albeit transfixed, until your mates pull you clear. Remember to keep hold of your axe.

CREVASSE ESCAPE/RESCUE

It can happen to the best of us, look here:

'We dossed disconsolately all the next day. The following day four of us agreed to go back up to Col Cave to retrieve the food and

134

equipment we had left there. It mostly belonged to Carl and Dave but Rob and I saw it as a way to while away the time. Our pilot wasn't due for another two days. It was fun to be on skis again, strange to be back at the Col. We found the cave exactly as we had left it. The weather looked as if it was worsening so we hurried away with huge loads. Going back down the glacier, a rope of four, I found myself appointed front man. I found a crevasse and fell in. And again, and again. Five times, once by twenty feet or so. There was no real danger; the other three held me easily, but it was annoying and unnerving. Every time it happened I crawled out angrier than the last, shouting that it was time someone else took a turn at the front – and stomping off again before anyone could do so.

'I didn't know it at the time but the other three were enjoying it all enormously. When we regained the place we had left our skis Carl came up with a huge grin and said in his drawl, a drawl so slow you wondered if the sentence would escape his mouth. "John, you're really beautiful when you're angry." The anger vanished, fled in an instant. We all laughed uproariously.' (*The Great Climbing Adventure.*)

Many climbers survive their entire alpine careers without once visiting the inside of a crevasse. Falling into a crevasse can be an unnerving experience but it is seldom a

Fig 132 Practising prusiking at home. The lengths of the respective prusik loops should be tailored to suit your own needs at waist and foot.

Fig 133 Some prefer a two-footed loop.

Fig 134 *On finding yourself in a crevasse first attach both prusik loops, or, if they are already attached deploy them.*

(a)

(b)

serious one – provided that your party is correctly roped and accoutred, with ice-axes, those prusik loops and all. Often, your fall having been quickly arrested by your alert and competent comrades, you will be able, very easily, to climb out in a matter of minutes. If the sides are too steep to climb (and sometimes they are overhanging, especially at the lip), or if you have inadvertently dropped your axe, there are a number of ways in which your partner or partners can help you. Indeed, if there were more than four on the rope in the first place there is a good chance that they will simply be able to turn around and, walking in the opposite direction, pull you out like the champagne cork I mentioned earlier. However, let's look at less simple situations, one step at a time.

It is essential that you know how to prusik up a rope (also *see* page 139), and though this is a fairly simple procedure, it is

Fig 135 (a) and (b) *Clip the shorter loop into your waist (if not already clipped) and stand in the longer with one or both feet. Continue to the top. Prusiking while hanging free like this, and such as you would hang in some crevasses (see Fig 97), is much harder work than if you can get a foot or feet, especially when cramponed, against the walk of a crevasse.*

one that is worth practising before you find yourself in a crevasse. Few alpinists bother, which is perhaps why so many make a hash of a simple thing, when confronted with the need.

Holding the fall is easier than you might think, especially in soft snow when it is relatively easy to dig yourself in, even though you are likely to be pulled off balance and dragged some way toward the slot into which you mate has fallen . An uphill fall is much easier to hold than a downhill fall. Three or more on the rope make this much easier than if there are only two, and it is easier too if the victim has fallen into a crevasse in front of you rather than behind.

The immediate reaction to one of the team falling in a crevasse is to throw yourself down on the snow − you may well be there already − and to dig in with feet, axe and, if necessary, hands and arms. Once you have succeeded in holding the fall (assuming a rope of two) and you are confident that you can remain in that position for some time, then that's all you have to do, until your partner emerges under his own steam. If you are in any doubt about your ability to stay in position, you should construct a belay as described below.

Fig 136   Prusiking with other than a light sack on the back is strenuous and it is much better to lower your centre of gravity by either dangling the sack below you on a sling attached to your harness at back or side, or, better still, clipping the sack into the climbing rope (on which you are prusiking), below your prusik loops.

Fig 137   The sack will then hang beneath you, counter-weighing directly on the rope, rather than on you, making it much easier for you to slide the prusik knots at each upward move.

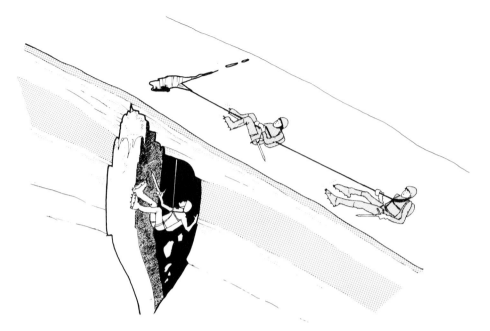

Fig 138 Uphill crevasse falls are easier to hold than . . .

Fig 139 . . . downhill falls.

Fig 140   Holding on and cutting.

You may be able to talk or shout to your partner. If he is all right, thinks he can climb out under his own steam and can communicate all this to you, all well and good. The difficulties begin when he announces that he is unable to climb out, or when you can't communicate with him at all. In the last case wait a few minutes to feel if he begins to prusik. If he does this you will be aware of his movements being transmitted through the rope and again all you need do is wait. If, however, after a few moments, nothing is happening then you may as well begin the next step, which is to construct a belay. In theory this is simple; in practice it is hard

Fig 141   Mick Woolridge demonstrates how to hold a crevasse-bound partner and cut a belay slot at the same time. Since this was a demonstration he has insured the show by investing in additional 'just in case' anchors – the ropes to which can be seen running out of the bottom of the picture. These are not, however, playing any other role.

work. Half-sitting, half-lying, take an axe and cut a slot behind you, big enough to accommodate at least an axe and preferably a rucksack; and deep enough to be in firm snow.

This is tiring work but don't be tempted to short cut; the integrity of the remainder of the rescue procedure depends on this single anchor and any reinforcement you can supply. Once the slot is big enough and deep enough for a good anchor, free the longer prusik loop (it should already be attached at one end to the rope) (*see* Fig 118), attach the other end to a sling with a karabiner and a mariner's knot and clove-hitch the sling to the shaft of the ice-axe or pass it around the centre of the body of the sack. (It is unlikely that even the long prusik will comfortably reach the buried axe without the sling extension, so make sure you have a sling and karabiner handy.) It is better to construct an anchor using a rucksack in the place of the ice-axe, and though this takes a bigger hole and is a little more difficult to attach the prusik, needing a longish sling to be sure of encircling the body of the sack, it makes for greater security in the long run.

Bury the axe or sack (with prusik attached via sling) deep and firm, patting, thumping and stamping on the filling so that the snow in which that axe is now incarcerated is *at least* as firm as the snow surrounding you. Keep at this until you are sure (and maybe exhausted). Now slide the prusik knot down the rope (on which you are still holding all the victim's weight) until the prusik loop is as tight between knot and anchor as you can make it. Then ease yourself forward so that the weight is gently transfered from you to the anchor via the prusik loop. You may now untie the climbing rope from your harness, effectively escaping from the system. You can remove the coils from your shoulder at the same time. This will give you spare rope with which to complete the next part of the rescue (or you can take out the spare rope – provided that it is not in the rucksack you have chosen to bury, or your partner's!).

As a precaution against the rope slipping through the prusik, tie a figure of eight knot above it as a stopper or better, clip the figure of eight into the anchor (*see* Fig 145(b)). Remain lying on the anchor so that you can check how it is bearing the strain. Take this opportunity to strengthen it all by further compressing the snow around it and tamping in more, but be careful not to disturb the integrity of the anchor.

The main load-bearing part of the entire system is the wall of the slope that you have cut nearest the victim. This wall is important: it should be slightly overhung if possible, and certainly no less than vertical. It should be square to the rescue area, and cleanly cut and as round as possible. Tamping the rucksack anchor serves as additional security, for, though it probably adds little to the overall strength of the anchor, it ensures that the anchors will not move, slide, tilt or skew – all of which could prove disastrous.

Once you have perfected the anchor, move carefully towards the edge of the crevasse until you can communicate with your mate. If you are in any doubt as to what is and what is not terra firma, then abseil toward the edge of the crevasse (yes, even on the horizontal) secured to a seperate anchor if you have sufficient rope and implements. (If there are three in your party, you will have already been able to do this with half the effort.) Even if the ground looks sound, if you have to go to the very edge it is as well to give yourself some security, either by tying in to the same anchors with the spare rope supplied by your removed coils,

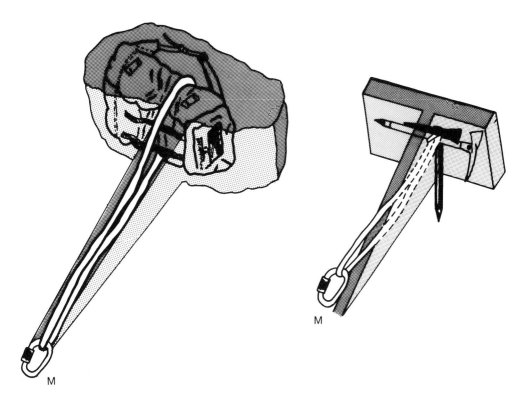

*Fig 142   Anchors fashioned with a rucksack and with two axes in 'T'
formation. If you have been carrying only one axe, or, having two, for
some reason – such as for cutting a slot at the lip of the crevasses (see Fig
154), or for reinforcing the snow against the rope (see Fig 151) – you
decide to retain the second axe and, which will be rare, you have no
rucksack, then your anchor will have to be made with a single axe planted
horizontally. Later, when you have finished with the second axe you can
use it to reinforce the first by inserting it verically and in front, to complete
the 'T'. Note that in this illustration the vertical axe, inserted as the anchor
was being fashioned, is behind the horizontal axe. This is generally
considered to be the stronger arrangement, especially when a clove-hitch
encircles both axes as it does here. A prusik can now be joined to the sling
via a karabiner and a mariner's knot at M. If you clip the prusik loop into
the karabiner without using a mariner's knot it will be difficult to release
under load once you have installed an autoblock – the next stage. You
could, of course, cut the prusik loop away with a knife once the autoblock
is in position, but that is an expensive solution and an unnecessary one
when a simple mariner's knot (see Appendix III) will do the job perfectly
well. (See pages 144 and 145.)*

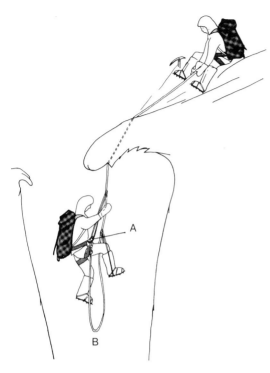

Fig 143 'Nine times out of ten your partner, if uninjured, should be able to prusik out'. A heavy rucksack is best suspended from the harness — at almost any point, but the front tie-in is perhaps the most convenient place (A) or it may be slung on the loop (B) that forms as you begin to ascend, and where it will also serve as a counterweight, making the business of prusiking somewhat easier than if that same weight remained on your back.

or by arranging a second anchor from a second axe, or, if so far unused, your rucksack. You may then safeguard yourself as far as to the edge of the crevasse until you can look over, preferably from a kneeling or lying position, to measure the problem. Another way to safeguard such a reconnaissance is to attach yourself to the loaded rope by means of a prusik to your harness and sliding this along behind you as you move toward the lip of the crevasse.

Fig 144 The assisted hoist — assisted, that is, by the victim who has, after all, a vested interest in the proceedings! The victim pulls down on P while the rescuer heaves up on H. The knot at AB is now an autoblock, which has replaced the original prusik, the rescuer having followed the sequence shown on page 144.

Nine times out of ten, your partner, if uninjured, should be able to climb or to prusik out. If he can't then there are two good ways in which you can assist him.

The Assisted Hoist

In this procedure the rope is arranged at the anchor as shown. (Note particularly the addition and positioning of the autoblock — see also page 144.) The original prusik can now be removed, thanks to the interposed mariner's knot, and the victim's weight transferred to the autoblock. The loop,

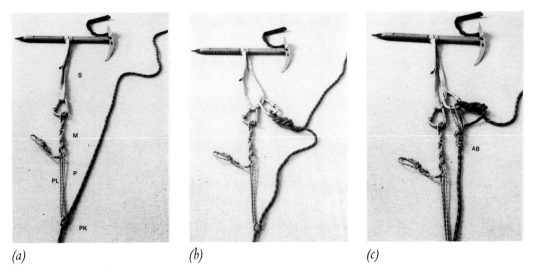

(a)   *(b)*   *(c)*

Fig 145 Crevasse escape: anchoring a victim. (a) The climbing rope is linked to the anchor (in this case a single axe) via a prusik knot (PK) and a prusik loop (PL) – standard glacier travel precautions – a mariner's knot (M), and a sling or slings. You can now untie from the climbing rope so that you may accomplish the succeeding steps as quickly as possible. (b) A figure of eight has been clipped into a karabiner and joined to the sling, as insurance against slippage through the prusik. (c) Introduce an autoblock (AB) when all has been checked and tightened.

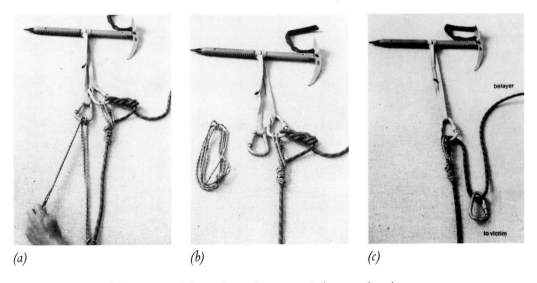

(a)   *(b)*   *(c)*

Fig 146 Assisted hoist. (a) and (b): Release the mariner's knot so that the victim's weight is now taken by the autoblock. (c) Clip a karabiner on to the rope above the autoblock and lower it on a bight to your partner.

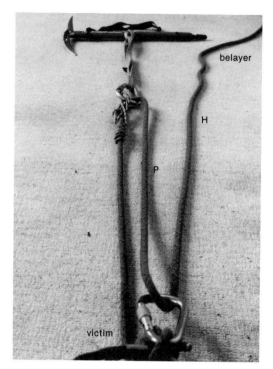

Fig 147 Assisted hoist. He clips it into his harness – almost anywhere will do. The belayer (rescuer) pulls on H with might; the victim on P with main! The autoblock insurers insures against the belayer accidentally letting go of the rope and allows rests to be taken without ground being lost. It is possible to achieve the same mechanics – though not quite as good results – by leaving the original prusik in position, foregoing the autoblock (the geometry of which may have deserted you in a crisis) and passing the rope through the karabiner holding the mariner's knot, or better, the one holding the back-up figure of eight knot. The advantage of an autoblock is that it works on its and does not need to be continually resited, though it does necessitate the replacement and removal of the original prusik. Relying on the original prusik saves replacement time and trouble, but it needs to be attended. If you are three, one could attend such a prusik; if two, you'll do better on a mariner's, and that little extra time will be well invested.

Fig 148 Detail of the autoblock.

with karabiner attached, is lowered (either by yourself if you are two, or, if you are more, by a third) to the victim. If he is able to help himself but unable to climb out unassisted – either because it is too steep, or because he has lost his axe or forgotten his prusiks – he clips the karabiner to his harness (for example, via the tie-in loop) and climbs with feet and whatever else he can muster while you (or a third member) pull from above.

The autoblock automatically and without being constantly tended, as would be the case with a simple prusik, safeguards the victim should the rope slide through your hands, and also so that you can take a breather without returning the victim precipitously to his low point. You in fact gain some mechanical advantage using this method – 2:1 or thereabouts – and the

144

Fig 149   Teams of alpinists practise crevasse rescue. It would have been more realistic had they chosen a snow-covered glacier to practise on – falling accidentally into a crevasse on a dry glacier takes some doing. Nevertheless, it is perhaps a good way in which to sort out the basic mechanics before graduating to the greater reaslism of a snow-covered glacier.

effort involved is not as great as it might appear. Nevertheless, it is one of those things that becomes easier with a little practice and which is, indeed, worth practising.

So the stages, arresting to assisted hoisting are:

1. Hold the fall (*see* Figs 140 and 141).
2. Fashion anchor (*see* Fig 142).
3. Attach a sling to that anchor (clove-hitched to a T-axe, or looped around a rucksack – *see* Fig 142).
4. Connect a prusik (already attached to a climbing rope) to the sling via a karabiner and mariner's knot (*see* Fig 145(a)). Anchor and prusik are now joined by sling, karabiner and mariner's knot.

5. Untie from the rope.
6. Back up the anchor with a figure of eight knot (*see* Fig 145(b)).
7. Decide, after a recce, whether to employ an assisted, simple unassisted or improved hoist and set this up, positioning an autoblock at AB (*see* Fig 145(c)). This is best done by clipping a second karabiner into the sling – the first will be getting congested with the prusik, autoblock and later rope. (*See* Figs 145(c), 147, 150, 153).
8. Release the mariner's knot, leaving the autoblock (*see* Fig 146(a)).
9. Release back up.
10. Proceed with rescue operation.

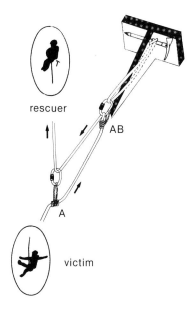

Fig 150 Detail of a simple unassisted
hoist. AB is the autoblock that has replaced
the original prusik (see Figs 145(a) and
148). A is a new prusik knot (a prusik is
satisfactory here since its only function is to
grip). You have now consumed 2 of 3 prusik
loops that you have been recommended to
carry. The arrows indicate the direction of
pull and of rope movement.

Fig 151 Simple unassisted hoist. Note that
the lip of the crevasse has been reinforced by
an axe. More likely this would be a piece of
karrimat or an article of clothing; it is
unlikely that you'd have three axes at your
disposal – and two have already been used
here in belaying.

(a)

(b)

Fig 152 (a) and (b) A simple pulley.

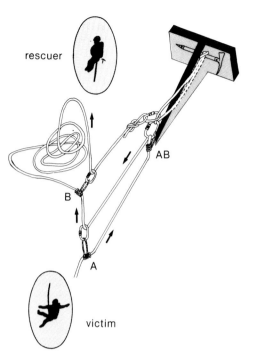

rescuer

AB

B

A

victim

Fig 153 The improved unassisted hoist. In essence all this 'improvement' consists of is a third prusik knot at B and a joining of an end, or bight, of rope at AB. This increases your mechanical advantage over the simple hoist by about 30 per cent.

The Simple Unassisted Hoist

If your partner is hanging free and is for some reason (such as injury, or loss of prusiks) unable to prusik out of the crevasse, it is unlikely that the assisted hoist will offer sufficient mechanical advantage to enable you to help him out. Even if he has use of his legs, hanging free he will be unable to reach anything on which to get a purchase. In these circumstances you will have to rig a hoist that affords sufficient advantage to pull him out directly and unassisted by the victim. If you were doing your job properly before the mishap occured he should not have fallen far into the crevasse (10 – 15ft at the most) and even in the worst case it is

Fig 154 Preparing the lip. Whenever you can, cut out a box at the lip of the crevasse to ease the passage of the rope around that corner. Reinforce the lip too, if possible. Sometimes lips of crevasses are overhanging and then it is best to cut a body-wide slot right through the overhang before arranging things as shown here. Protect yourself by tying into the anchor via the climbing rope first: the idea is that your mate should join you – not the other way around! Clearly this is time-consuming, as well as tiring, but it may otherwise prove impossible to hoist your mate over the lip.

unlikely that all of that distance will be so overhanging that he can't get his feet to something before too long. As with the previous system some earlier rehearsal is recommended; it is much simpler in practice than the simplest drawing can make it appear – and speed is important, as crevasses are cold places to linger.

The anchor for the simple unassisted hoist is established in exactly the same way as for the assisted hoist: escaping from your rope too. Then arrange things as in Fig 150.

In practice the friction generated by the rope running over the edge of the crevasse, even when that edge has been cut away (Fig 154) and reinforced with clothes, rucksack or ice-axe, combined with the friction generated by the same rope's passage through two karabiners in opposite directions, makes it almost impossible for one person to make any headway in pulling in the rope – although you'll fare much better with a team of three.

If this is the case you can do one of four things:

1.   Persevere with the struggle.
2.   Use a small pulley in place of at least one of the karabiners. This is a practical enough solution since such pulleys exist for precisely that purpose, and they are cheap, very light in weight and easy to use. However, I have never known other than professional mountain guides make a habit of carrying one – though that is no reason why we all should not.
3.   Double up karabiners at both turns. This reduces the friction because the radius around which the rope runs is much wider.
4.   Invest in greater mechanical advantage by establishing an improved unassisted hoist. This will take prior practice.

Once established, life will be easy, and very elephants will be plucked from nethermost crevasses with ease.

Note: Two tips for making all forms of crevasse rescue easier:

1.   Chop a box from the lip of the crevasse so that the rope lies against a wall rather than running itself into a tight slot. This will both avoid friction between rope and slot and give the victim a much easier exit. Be very careful, however, not to strike the rope with the axe: a rope taut with the weight of a climber will readily cut and part with alarming ease.
2.   Always reinforce the edge of the crevasse with clothing, a rucksack or a spare axe, if one of these is available.

Unconscious Victim

If the victim of the crevasse fall is unconscious, things are considerably more serious. Given that there are sufficient members in the party, or if others are close enough to be pressed into service, the victim should he hauled out as quickly as possible and first aid administered. If he cannot be immediately hauled out then someone should abseil in to give first aid *in situ*. Then you'll have to prusik out and establish an improved hoist. It will be readily appreciated how quickly the time is being consumed and how cold an unconscious victim will be growing. Speed and efficiency are important and only to be learned, again, through practice. It will certainly be worth spending a rest day or a day when poor weather has counselled against going on the hill in playing at crevasse rescue in earnest.

In the worst case where you simply cannot hoist up an injured victim by yourself you will have to tie him off, having first administered any necessary first aid and wrapped as much spare clothing around him as possible, and go for help to the nearest hut or valley base.

Crossing glaciers is a serious business, but not, in most circumstances, a dangerous one, especially if properly practised, prepared and equipped.

5 All-Round Alpine Skills

In this chapter I propose to cover those climbing techniques which are unique to alpinism. All your previous climbing experience will be brought to bear in the alps, be it on rock or snow, or both. Most of that experience will travel well and once differences in scale and altitude have been adjusted to, you'll naturally apply it to alpine terrain with only the slightest of modification. There are, however, a handful of skills that are not commonly learned at home on rock outcrops or at winter climbing playgrounds. It is these and their modifications that I wish to dwell on. Most of them exist in the interests of greater speed, this being a great alpine virtue.

A number of factors contribute to speediness:

1. Physical fitness.
2. Acclimatisation.
3. Accurate route finding.
4. Good rope management – moving together at every opportunity.
5. The minimum of halts (whether for rest, food or re-organisation).
6. Overcoming obstacles quickly.

The first two have already been dealt with; 5 and 6 come of care and experience. Numbers 3 and 4 deserves detailed attention.

ROUTE FINDING

It is important to be able to find the way on an alpine rock climb because there may be a wide variety in the technical difficulty of two only slightly different lines – as there may be on any home-based crag. Trade routes are usually well labelled – slings, pegs, tins, chocolate papers and other human waste; less popular routes are not usually so well labelled. Some tips are:

1. Glean a thorough knowledge of the route from all possible sources – guidebooks, photographs, maps, articles etc. If you have access to a photograph, perhaps a better one than is shown in the guidebook, then take it (Fig 179). Likewise a topo – which you could also trace or photocopy.

Fig 155   The mark of stonefall: expended missles on the Eiger's North Face.

149

2.   Take the easiest line, to begin with at any rate, and avoid unnecessary technical hardships which will waste time and energy. Later in your alpine career, if you're hell-bent on immortality, you can take the hardest line you can find, but until then, if you find that the climbing is appreciably harder than the guidebook has suggested, then you're probably off-route. If that happens, stop and sniff around the corner; corners often hide easier lines. Try to correlate what the guidebook says you have, or should have climbed, with what you know you have climbed. All part of the Divine Mystery of the Oromaniacal Quest!

3.   Watch any parties ahead of you. They may not be right, but you should learn something, even if that something is only that they are wrong; at least that is one possible error eliminated.

4.   Tins, pegs and footmarks are better signposts than bits of paper which may have blown in from another route. Beware *pitons d'erreur*, however. They are sometimes recognisable by a solitary piece of abseil sling and a solitary look. Pitons that are frequently abseiled from (which *pitons d'erreur* ought not to be) are usually festooned in abseil tape.

PITONS

Pitons and wedges (and now bolts) are sited far more generously in alpine rock than on most domestic crags. And generally speaking they are there to use: to pull on, stand on, stand in, sling on – or whatever is expedient. This is mainly because there is less time available to unlock the secret of an intricate move – though you are, of course, entirely free to apply ethics as rigorous as you feel inclined.

Generally speaking, pitons on alpine routes are already *in situ*. Don't ponder the moral issues, use them or ignore them according to disposition, and leave them for others to do the same. You really need only carry pitons of your own when you have graduated to harder routes (which may, indeed, not take very long) and even then a range of nuts is often to be preferred, being lighter to carry and quicker to use (*see* kit list on page 65).

ROPE MANAGEMENT AND MOVING TOGETHER

The method for roping up for alpine climbing is the same as for most other kinds of climbing, that is, via a sit-harness (*see* page 54) tied into the climbing rope. Steep, technical ground, whether rock, snow or ice, or mixed, is climbed pitch by pitch, belaying and placing runners in exactly the same way as you would at home – except that you are likely to have on your back a heavier rucksack than you would be used to – if, indeed, you are used to one at all. It is not on this technical ground where the alpine differences are to be found but on the easy to moderate ground that comprises the far greater part of all but the hardest alpine routes. On these sorts of terrain the idea is to move together whenever possible – a practice which more than halves the time it would take to 'pitch' the same distance. At first you may find this unnerving, or awkward, especially with a new partner. Your confidence, however, will grow rapidly with experience and you'll soon find yourself eating up alpine miles. When moving together, the members of the party (usually two, but it could be three or more) should normally move 15–30ft apart

(a)   (b)   (c)

Fig 156   (a) to (c): Take in neat coils, 4 or 5 should be enough. So that the coils do not continually slip through your hand as you climb, secure them by taking the last coil around the back of the remainder before grasping in the hand.

(a)   (b)   (c)

Fig 157   (a) to (c): The resultant formation should be held as shown in (a). The coils may be swapped from hand to hand as the lie of the land dictates. When swapping try to ensure that you transfer the complete package, securing loop and all.

though this varies according to terrain and convenience: it could be less, it will sometimes be more. The rope should be shortened by taking in coils and tying off as for glacier travel. But there is one important difference: when moving together on the mountain (that is off glaciated and, therefore, un-crevassed terrain) all members of the party will carry two or three coils in one hand. (Note too that no crevasses means no prusik loops.)

The skill lies in dropping and retaking those coils according to the relative speed of party members, which is largely dictated by the ground over which an individual is travelling – and which may not be the same as that over which you are travelling 20 feet in front, or behind. The leader chooses the line, perhaps dropping his hand coils when he comes to a difficult step that demands both his hands. At the same time the second, whose job it is to manage the rope and see to it that it doesn't catch or snarl, on seeing the leader drop his hand coils, may also drop his own and take up a direct belay (*see* page 155). Then the leader, having overcome the difficulty, may secure the second by a direct belay from above, before they both retake hand coils and move off as before. A well-knit team will need to

Fig 158 A team, moving together on a shortened rope, has decided that the next section of (in this case) ridge is too tricky to be negotiated simultaneously, so, dropping hand coils, one has taken a handy direct belay on a sling dropped over an even handier spike and secured himself to the same anchor, while the other forges ahead. If the distance between anchors, or between anchor and easy ground, is longer than the rope made available by purely the release of both sets of hand coils, then one or both climbers may have to release torso coils too. All these should be retaken when next convenient.

Fig 159 Struggling to manage rope (and rope and rope and rope) in an Alaskan storm on Mt. Deborah.

exchange few words beyond whatever pleasantries are already passing (it is to be hoped) between them.

Because of the great distances involved a team of alpinists should move together whenever possible. Their willingness and ability to do this depends on:

1. Individual abilities within the party.
2. Good judgement as to what is safe ground over which to move together and what is not. The latter may include technically difficult ground, bad rock, verglas, dangerous snow and rotten ice.
3. Their skill in rope management.
4. The alertness of the party.

Points to watch are:

1. Keep the rope between climbers snugly taut at all times.
2. Be diligent in taking in and letting out coils as necessary, so that the rope never lies on the ground or catches in rocks or loose stones; and so that a slip is no longer than it need be.
3. Maintain a steady rhythm that all can hold to.
4. Avoid rushing when on easy ground – your mate may still be grappling with an obstacle.
5. When on a ridge try to have one member just on the other side, (but not when there's a cornice). When so arranged slips down one side or the other are easy to hold.
6. If you are all necessarily on the crest of a ridge be alert to a slip and be prepared to

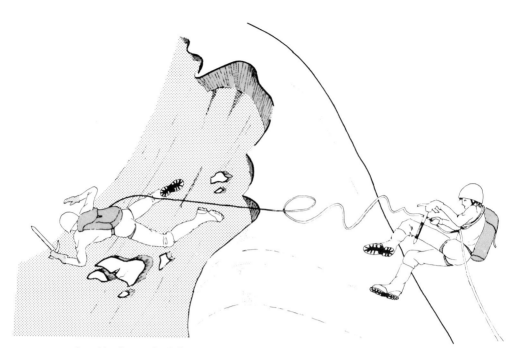

Fig 160 'The old joke, "If I fall into France, you jump into Italy"'. If a cornice collapses under your colleague – and in a prudent team only one of its members would be standing into danger at any one time – then you may have to take fairly drastic remedial action like dashing (or throwing yourself) down the other side. Whether you take your leave to France or Italy, your hand coils will almost certainly be snatched away – most certainly in a tumble as dramatic as the one illustrated here. Hang on to your axe – if your mates have done their job, you'll be needing it again soon.

jump to the other side. (Hence the old joke on the Rochefort Arête, the frontier ridge between France and Italy: 'If I fall into France, you jump into Italy.')

7. Be prepared for direct belays when the difficulties suggest them. But resume moving together as soon as possible.

Running Belays When Moving Together

Snow/Ice

The most usual running belay when moving together across or up a snow slope is the ice-axe itself, which is not so much a running belay, as a mobile one. On a traverse, for example, the climbers will travel with the axe held in the uphill hand (that is, the hand nearest the slope). The coils will usually be carried in the downhill hand. In the event of a slip the ice-axe is plunged shaft-first into the snow and, if possible – and this does take some practice – the rope is hitched around the shaft at snow level before it tightens on the shaft. The belaying climber then hurls his weight over the axe.

On Rocky or Mixed Terrain

The leader keeps an eye open for any spikes or bollards over which he may drape a sling,

Fig 161   Foot brake. To hold a slip or tumble, move the belaying hand — in this case, the left hand behind the right foot. The line rope will then describe an 'S' shape, around axe-shaft and ankle, providing sufficient friction to arrest the sort of shock load that might be expected from a stumble on non-technical ground. This is the sort of ground on which you might employ a foot brake in order to safeguard one another over a short obstacle. The axe should be held firmly into the snow, especially in névé.

which attached to the rope by a karabiner, provides a quick and effective running belay. He may shape as many runners in this fashion as he feels the need of security for. The second collects them as he follows. A practised team can place and collect runners in this way almost without breaking step. When the leader's supply of slings is exhausted he will need to stop until his second brings up the re-supply. And away they go again. On ridges and across very broken ground a certain degree of security can be won from deliberately weaving the rope in and out of boulders, natural snow bollards and other outcrops.

DIRECT BELAYS

Moving singly, unroped is the fastest, but least secure way of covering alpine ground. Moving together, roped is the next fastest — and, well practised and well conducted, this can be both a speedy and a safe way to travel. Before we slow to full pitch by pitch, belay by belay, climbing — as will indeed be necessary on the hardest of alpine routes — there is an intermediary stage, between moving together and full-pitching. This involves direct belaying. It can be used in the last stage of moving together or in the first stages of climbing by pitches — or indeed as the means of belaying even when climbing by pitches.

The 'direct' bit of the phrase means that the rope runs directly from the climber to the belay anchor without passing around the belayer as would be the more conventional case. Direct belays are more commonly used to protect the second man rather than the leader, although in some circumstances a properly secured direct belay will adequately protect a leader too.

The Italian hitch (shown in Appendix III) is a useful knot in all direct belays, whilst belay plates such as the Sticht, can also be used directly.

Direct Belays on Rock

In practice and with experience direct belays can be used on the hardest of alpine routes. They should not be used, however, if the anchor to which the direct belay is secured is at all suspect. In this case a conventional body belay should be employed with the belayer interposing himself between belay anchor and belayed, and so reducing the shock load that might otherwise be borne direct by the anchor in the event of a fall.

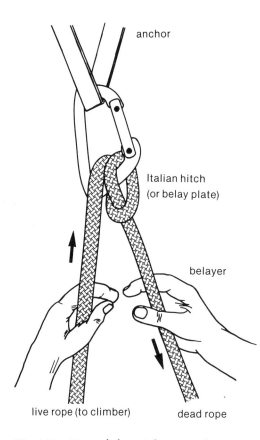

anchor

Italian hitch
(or belay plate)

belayer

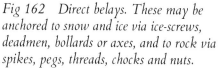

live rope (to climber)   dead rope

*Fig 162   Direct belays. These may be
anchored to snow and ice via ice-screws,
deadmen, bollards or axes, and to rock via
spikes, pegs, threads, chocks and nuts.*

This applies especially to leader falls where
the energy generated will nearly always be
far greater than that of a fall by a second.

If in any doubt, and certainly when
climbing near your limit – unlikely in your
first season – belay conventionally. The
cost in time may be a good investment.

Direct belaying and conventional belaying can be usefully combined and converted
as follows:

1.   The leader, on gaining a stance,
establishes a direct belay through which he
brings up the second.

2.   The second has no need to seek an
anchor but merely inherits that of the
leader, into which he quickly clips by
converting the leader's Italian hitch into a
clove hitch, which anchors the second
immediately.

3.   He then takes the leader on a new
Italian hitch from a karabiner attached to his
harness or belay plate used direct, or in a
conventional body belay if that is preferred.

MORE ON BELAYING

The full range of conventional belays,
whether in rock or in snow or ice, are likely
to be called upon in the alps at some stage –
pegs, nuts, chocks, threads, ice screws,
snargs (especially good in alpine winter ice),
deadmen (if they are carried, 'which is
seldom), snow and ice bollards, buried T-
axes – they are all part of the alpinist's
safety repertoire.

Some alpinists carry a sturdy sling permanently clipped into their harness (at a strong
point such as the tie-in loop – or, less
comfortably, around the waist belt). A
second karabiner lives on the sling. When
arriving at a belay all the climber has to do is
remove the sling from a shoulder and pass it
over a spike, or clip the second karabiner
into an *in-situ* peg. In this way adequate
belays can be made without tying any knots.

Give some thought to your systems of
belaying – they must be safe and quick to
establish, change over or inherit; not a
combination that can be achieved without
consideration and experimentation.

Leading Through

Leading through (swinging leads) will probably not save as much time in the alps as it does on climbs at lower altitudes, unless both climbers are very fit and well acclimatised. One rope length climbed rapidly at 4,000m is often enough, especially with rucksack and other paraphernalia, so that by the time the second has joined the leader he may feel disinclined to launch out immediately on another 45m of strenuous climbing. Nor will he have had as much time as the leader to spy out the way ahead. Most parties will find it more satisfactory to swap the lead every 6 to 10 pitches instead. Hence the importance of slick belay swaps; there will be 6 to 10 in every change of lead and each is a potential time-water.

Sack Hauling

With the modern approach to hard alpine rock climbing (*see* Chapter 7), sack hauling is dying a natural death, which is no loss since it was a fairly laborious and a joyless performance anyway. It should hardly ever be necessary to sack haul in your first season and only ever be necessary on steep, hard rock or on very steep ice. One way to avoid it — it's time consuming and fraught with inconveniences — on hardish climbs is for the leader to climb with a lighter sack, the second with a heavier. The sacks can be exchanged with leads.

If you do resort to hauling, use a separate rope and, if possible, tie the sack on in the middle of it so that the second can help to control its ascent from below. Hauled sacks have a penchant for jamming in chimneys, under flakes, and about anywhere else that never seemed likely. Most modern climbing sacks have a haul loop sewn into the top.

Ice-axes and crampons are best stowed inside a sack that is to be hauled. On the whole it is better to go light and fast if that is possible.

MOVING ON SNOW AND ICE – FURTHER THOUGHTS

Alpine climbing involves movement on snow and ice of all steepnesses, from spirit-level flat to plump vertical, even odd overhanging bits. Moreover, conditions vary enormously, not so much day to day as they do in, say, Scotland, but within the span of a day – forenoon to afternoon – and this is an especially important consideration in descents, many of which take place mid-afternoon. There are the objective dangers to ponder too, such as avalanche and stonefall, that have already been dealt with. There are several points to ponder.

Avalanche Snow·

Avalanche danger can be minimised by:

1. Keeping to the rocks when the snow arises suspicion or by linking rock to rock when dangerous snow must be crossed. Fig 163 shows the sort of choice that you might face and traces a possible solution.
2. Keeping as high as possible, moving one at a time, belayed from a safe position.
3. Avoiding lee slopes after storms – they will be prone to windslab.
4. Old avalanche troughs sometimes make for safe lines; the danger having departed. Furthermore, the snow in an old avalanche trough may be a lot easier to walk and climb on to than shin-deep afternoon porridge.

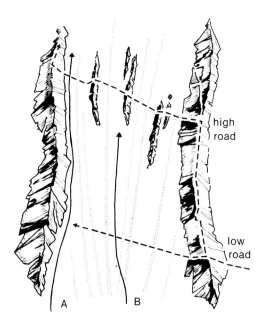

Fig 163   Minimising avalanche danger by choosing the best line in a couloir. When climbing or descending, A is safer than B because: (i) snow is less likely to avalanche where it borders the rock – and even if it does it will move more slowly; (ii) you can hang on to something of terra firma; (iii) you will have been able to find – and use – good anchors and runners. When crossing, the high road is safer than the low road because: (i) the higher you are in a couloir that does avalanche the less snow there will be above to bury you; (ii) in this case there are islands of rock; islands, too, of safety. Should nature not be so considerate as to sprinkle her rocks across the top of a couloir, but lay them instead across a lower reach, then you have to toss up between factors (i) and (ii).

But avoid troughs made by avalanches falling from somewhere above – there may be worse still to come.

Couloirs

These are wide gulleys and are usually snow or ice-filled and contained by rock walls. Many fine alpine routes lie up them: they show a short and direct way to summits. The Black Ice Couloir, Grand Teton, Wymoning; in the Mont Blanc range the Dru Couloir, the Gervasutti Couloir and, the Couturier Couloir; the Diamond Couloir on Mt Kenya – these are world-wide examples. But couloirs for all their elegance of line are natural channels for debris – for falling snow and ice and rocks. This is particularly so in the afternoons, by which time the sun will have warmed the upper reaches, even in couloirs of a northerly aspect. Then all that the sun has warmed will be loosened and may tumble.

Couloirs are usually dangerous places by mid-morning, certainly by midday (for example, the Whymper Couloir on the Aiguille Verte, notorious for its instability soon after the sun reaches it, in the early morning). Some couloirs are permanently dangerous because they are topped by seracs which may tumble at any time of the day or night. The Grand Couloir on the Brenva Face of Mont Blanc is an example: not a place to linger in the crossing; never a place to climb up or down. Some points to consider are:

1. If your planned route involves a couloir in ascent or descent, try to plan things so that you encounter it at a safe time, that is very early in the morning in ascent, as early as 1 a.m. perhaps, or later in the afternoon when it has lost the sun.
2. Keep close to the walls and use any shelter and belays that those walls provide (*see* Fig 163). Avoid the middle, especially if it is gouged by a 'rigole' – a channel cut by falling debris.

3.   A surface of hard frozen snow – névé – will make the going much easier. Soft snow is tiring and dangerous – and if it is soft in the early hours of the morning the weather is too warm and you'd be better off climbing elsewhere, on a ridge for example. Conversely, the hard black ice of late-season couloirs is hard work and unfriendly to climb on – though not avalanche prone. Once again you might be better advised to look elsewhere.

Cornices

These are common on alpine ridges the world over and even bigger in Alaska and the Andes than they are in the European Alps. Those who have cut their milk teeth on Scottish cornices will be surprised by

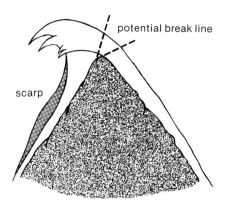

Fig 164   Cornices: the break line. If cornices break off it is usually along the continuation of the angle of the slope that they overhang. But it is possible that the break will be further back than that, so give them as wide a berth as is practical.

Fig 165   Smallish and relatively benign cornices on the Tromsdaltind in Arctic Norway.

Fig 166   A larger, less friendly summit cornice overhangs the E. face of Mt. Tasman (the snow peak in the foreground). Mt. Cook, the highest mountain of the Southern Alps of New Zealand towers behind.

their size and complexity: alpine cornices are frequently multi-layered and often double – a flange on either side. Double cornices are difficult to cross in safety and their pressure may enforce a retreat. Tracks of earlier parties are useful, but don't follow them blindly; that party may have trod in blissful ignorance and luck, and you may not be so lucky. It is hard to be certain where the potential break-line of a cornice is exactly. If in any doubt – and second and third men can often judge better than the first – give a cornice a wide margin on the safe side.

Nor are cornices good things to climb beneath. Here's a tale of a cornice collapsing on to the heads of Nicholls and me while we

were climbing a new route on the N. Face of the Aiguille de Leschaux near Courmayeur.

'For the most part the ice gave the line so we followed our noses and they rarely lied and though the ground steepened it was still all very reasonable. We were happy in our work and chatted cheerfully whenever we met. I led a pitch; drove in a peg and belayed. Dave came up, at the gallop, took some gear and led on. 'OK mate,' he yelled, meaning that he was belayed. I untied from my peg and began to knock it out when a steady roar caught my mind's ear. Leaving the peg I glanced around the cirque in the hope of a glimpse of something spectacular. Nothing doing. Returning to the peg I became aware of a darkening above. A quick look up. Damn! Dave had already seen it and was road-runner flat against the hill. The vision was quick, the impression quicker and the memory hazy but I recall huge blocks of ice and seemingly endless cascades of slow snow streaming off the summit slopes and out, out, out into the sky above us. Escape looked unlikely and too frightened to panic we cravenly cowered – and survived. Ice broke on rocks all about, but none on us while snow buffeted but left us attached until at last the sky cleared and the discovery that I was unscathed encouraged me to enquire after Nicholls. 'Dave, Dave, you OK?' No answer. Panic. How to get down . . . rescue . . . insurance . . . me?

'I'm OK, what will we do?' – a small voice miles off at 150 feet away. 'It's this bloody couloir.'

'Same up or down – and we're nearer the top,' I answered with half-hearted, half-convinced reason.

There being nothing more to say the rope went tight, I removed the peg and went on up to Dave. Together we were braver – though still very shaken. But it would be safer ahead, steeper and therefore safer, and in any case there was probably no more to come – we argued with a logic short on alternatives.'(*The Great Climbing Adventure*)

MOVEMENT ON ALPINE ROCK

I am confining myself here to the traditional approach to alpine rock, the approach indeed that still holds good to most of the remoter alpine regions of the world. Alpine rock climbing in the European Alps has undergone something of a revolution in the

last few years and this is dealt with in Chapter 7. So to the traditional approach which may be summarised as:

1.   Go as fast as is consistent with safety.
2.   Be economical with ethics (which may be your practice anyway!). Where a sling suggests speed, use it – and any other 'cheating' gambit you may have perfected on domestic crags. The aim is to get up and away home before the weather changes.
3.   Climb with your sack until you can't, then haul until you can.
4.   Encountering short rock pitches between ice, consider climbing on without removing crampons – though modern step-in bindings have made this practice less of a time-saver than of old.

THE DESCENT

Descents need special care; this is the time when accidents are most likely to occur. Points to watch are:

1.   Keep concentrating on route finding, footing, ropework, loose rock, etc.
2.   Scramble down as fast as is consistent with safety (again!) and scramble facing out (quicker and easier) until the angle persuades you to turn inwards. Steeper than that, abseil as explained in the following section.
3.   Beware poor snow conditions and balling crampons after mid-morning (*see* page 97), avalanches (*see* page 99), stonefall (*see* page 108) and weakened snow bridges (*see* page 133).
4.   Concentrate on concentrating when you have regained the glacier – it's not quite over yet. Keep roped for longer than seems necessary as a glacier changes from

snow-covered to dry. Not all the crevasses will be immediately visible (*see* page 115).

Abseiling/Rappeling

This is often necessary, especially on the more difficult rock climbs but on many easy climbs too. The unhappy fact is that abseiling is the major source of alpine accidents, with the causes about equally divided between mechanical failures (anchors failing, slings breaking) and human error – most abseiling takes place at the end of a day (or days) when climbers are hot and tired and anxious for the valley.

Abseil Anchors on Rock

Check them carefully. On most popular alpine routes abseil anchors will already be founded. Look at them. Are they good? Do they need to be reinforced? Is the *in-situ* tape good? The trouble with tape is that it degrades in ultraviolet light – of which there is a surfeit at alpine altitudes – and that old or nicked (that is slightly cut, not stolen!) tape, the sort that is often happily sacrificed to an abseil anchor is markedly weaker than new tape, sometimes fatally so. If you decide that the *in-situ* slings are good enough, or if you have none left of your own to reinforce them (or you can't afford to in any case) then at least pass your abseil

Fig 167 *Abseiling from the summit tower of the Meije. The climber had left his sack at the foot of the tower – but a few pitches from the top – to save himself time and weight. He'll collect it on return.*

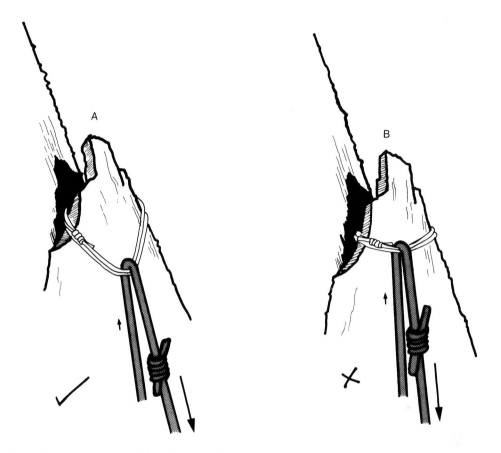

Fig 168   Ropes arranged for abseiling, showing which should be pulled in retrieval. A further refinement is to tie a reef-knot between the two sides of the double fisherman's, making it much easier to dismantle the knot after it has been tightened by abseiling (see Fig 172). Slings should not fit spikes too tightly. A tight sling is a weak one, and arranged as in B they have been known to fail.

rope through all that are available – and there may be half a dozen. It's worth carrying some spare tape or 5mm or 7mm line for such contingencies, and remember, join tape with a tape or waterman's knot, rope with a double fisherman's knot.

Check that *in-situ* pitons are sound, not too rusted or cracked and preferably at right angles to the direction of pull.

If you are arranging a sling around a spike or bollard from which to abseil ensure that the sling's circumference is comfortably greater than that of the spike. A tight sling is a weak one. Correctly established it should look like the one shown in Fig 168(a).

Whenever abseiling descend at a steady rate; bouncing and braking hard loads the anchor unnecessarily.

If the abseil rope jams as you attempt to retrieve it don't climb back up the rope (or

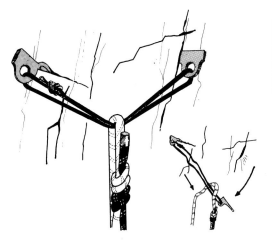

Fig 169   Pegs dangerously joined. Use separate slings in either peg and thread the abseil rope through each.

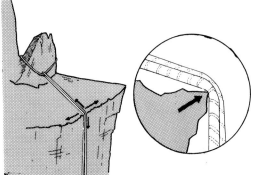

Fig 170   Avoid sharp edges. Even if the rope doesn't travel laterally across them, anything other than the smoothest abseil will cause it to alternately stretch and contract across it.

prusik) unless you still have both rope-ends to hand, and even then be sure that you prusik or climb gripping both ropes. A jam that occurs when the rope is half-pulled down cannot be depended on to hold your weight (which was how the great Gervasutti was killed). If this happens and you cannot free it by pulling, flicking or wrenching free, then you will either have to abandon the rope or climb up without its help to free it. A jammed abseil rope is a serious business and it's well worth investing time and energy to reduce the chances of this happening.

Whenever possible ensure that the ends of the abseil ropes can be seen, and that you can see too where that particular abseil ends, or at least a friendly ledge where you could stop and set up the next abseil. If you cannot see the ends of the ropes from your start point, or a disembarking point is not apparent, tie a knot (figure of eight) in the end of both ropes so that at least there is no danger of you abseiling off the end.

Always keep your prusik loops handy when abseiling so that should you find yourself in space at the end of the ropes and unable to gain any terra firma you can at least prusik back up and think again. If you are a less than confident abseiler you might have insured yourself by a prusik anyway or autoblock. Some advise that all abseiling should be reinforced in this way – it ensures against, in part, being hit by stonefall.

Always use a sling rather than risk passing the rope itself directly around a spike or block, a course that, nine times out of ten, results in so much friction that it will not be retrieved, or if it is at terrible cost to both arms and rope. You'll get away with this around a tree, but not much more – and there are precious few trees at alpine altitudes.

Beware stonefall which is almost as bad news for ropes (especially stretched, taut abseil ropes which are easily cut) as it is for climbers' heads.

A sequence for the setting up of an abseil might then be as follows:

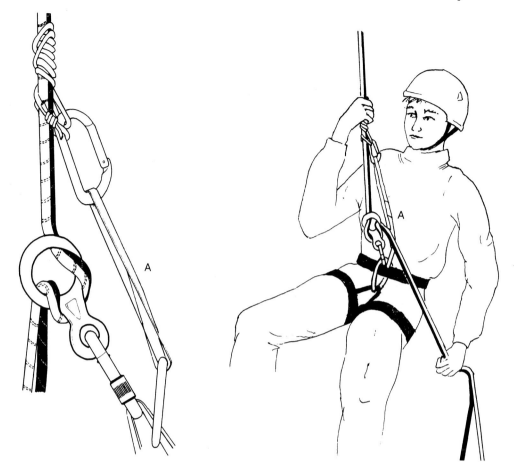

*Fig 171 Backing up an abseil with an autoblock. Beware though that it
doesn't grip, and then jam, prematurely. Freeing a jammed and loaded
friction knot whilst abseiling is an inconvenience you can do without. If it
does happen you may be able to take sufficient weight on your feet to allow
you to unload the knot enough to free it. If you are abseiling 'free' off the
rock, however, you will have little choice but to stand in a sling attached to
a second friction knot in order to free the first. It is better therefore to use
an autoblock than a prusik which can be freed whilst under load.*

1.   Select a safe anchor and check to see that
it is sound, visually, and if it's a block or
spike, by main. If the abseil looks to exceed
the length of a single rope doubled – about
20m – then join both ropes. This is best
done by first joining them with a reef knot
and then completing with a double fisher-

man's – an arrangement that is an improvement on the more usual double fisherman's on its own because the latter tightens
so much even after just a couple of abseils, as
to almost defy separation.
2.   But before joining the ropes, pass one
end through the anchor and then complete

165

the knot. This saves having to thread 45m of rope through the anchor after the ropes have been joined.

3.   Double check that:

(a) The ropes are indeed joined.

(b) A rope indeed passes through the anchor. This apparently insulting admonishment will stop you casting your entire supply of ropes to the 'twelve clean winds of heaven' – a lunacy that has been performed by more than one team of my acquaintance.

4.   Throw, feed or otherwise encourage the ropes down the mountain. This is not always the simple manoeuvre that it may sound. Strong winds are easily capable of bringing the rope back to you and the ropes themselves have an infuriating fondness for one another and the resultant embrace soon

Fig 172   Interpose a reef-knot between the two halves to make it easier to untie.

leads to a loving entwine and then an inextricable tangle.

5.   Once the ropes are lying in orderly fashion down the mountainside, clip in – a descendeur is recommended – and abseil away, under control. The first man down may have to clear tangles that he had not spotted from above. When he has reached the next stance (assuming that this abseil did not end on the ground) he can set about preparing the next anchor, and even pre-passing an end of rope through it if there is rope to spare. Not all abseils are necessarily the full length of the rope, and you may have deliberately stopped short at the last visible stance if the way ahead was not clear. Let your mate at the top know when you have unhitched from the abseil rope. If communication is difficult he should be able to gauge this by periodically testing the abseil rope with a pluck; it is obvious when the abseiler has alighted – or the first abseiler might use two strong and distinct tugs to signal that the rope is free. On other than a commodious stance, clip into the new anchor before releasing yourself from the abseil rope.

Before quitting the top the second man checks:

1.   Which rope should be pulled in order to retrieve the ropes (this might also have been noted by the first man on the abseil: two heads being better than one). If you are of fickle memory, shorter in span than the elapse of one abseil – and my own memory is frequently shorter even than that – then you can rig an idiot's *aid-mémoire* by clipping a karabiner into the recovery rope, above you. This serves no other purpose than to accompany you down the mountain in order to remind you at the other end

which rope you should pull. But whatever strategem you use to remember which rope it is you must pull, remember, because pulling the wrong rope simply doesn't work, and worse, by the time you have realised your mistake, you may have already jammed both ropes, irrevocably.

2. That the ropes will recover, by pulling down on the recovery rope to see if the system slides. If it doesn't he should make the necessary adjustments. These usually involve reducing friction.

Then (with maybe one last anxious look at the anchors) the second man abseils, also clipping into the new anchor at the bottom if necessary. Now you can both address yourselves to the recovery of the rope. In so far as you are able, check that the doubled abseil rope isn't twisted around itself, and, if it is, try to untangle it as well as you can before attempting to pull it down. Pull smoothly, hand over hand, four hands to the rope if necessary, until it falls free from the top anchor. At the same time the lower end of the recovery rope is fed through its new anchor (if not already begun) so that when the rope at last falls free from above, the new abseil is almost set and ready for use.

Check that all is well; that the anchor still looks good; that the ropes will run and which side the knot lies and which rope, therefore, is the recovery rope; that the ropes lie untangled below; and that there is a ledge or a landing to go for. And away you go again, for as many repetitions as will get you to the bottom.

Fig 173   Abseiling from a snow bollard. The last person to descend would have to take the ice axe that has been left here to strengthen the bollard. Bollards cut in ice need only be about a quarter of this size.

Note: A descendeur or belay plate (employed in an abseiling role) are worth the extra ounces carried for the greater comfort and security they afford in abseiling.

Abseil Anchors on Snow and Ice

It is possible to abseil from ice screws and from ice-axes and then to recover them, but none of the ways of doing these things are reliable and since having to abandon an ice-screw is expensive, and to abandon an ice-axe or rope potentially dangerous, then it is considered better to eschew them. Better instead to rely on snow or ice bollards as abseil anchors. They are dependable and

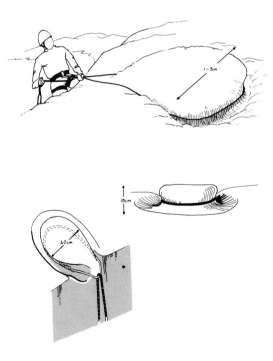

Fig 174   Snow and ice bollards: top, a bollard in snow; below, an ice bollard.

cheap and though they are time-consuming it is not often that the need arises.

BIVOUACS

I suspect that the great majority of alpine climbers have never bivouaced and never intend to. And you may be of that persuasion too. Even so, it is worth knowing something of the rudiments in case you are caught up in some emergency that entails a bivouac – it may be nothing more than that you were slower than you anticipated, or that you were more lost than you thought. Neither of those possibilities are, in themselves, very serious, and if rounded off by a tolerably comfortable bivouac, the whole may be a pleasant experience, a lovely unexpected dawn in new perspective, a tale to tell, a memory to cherish. Bivouacs are no great things in reasonable circumstances; in favourable circumstances they are a delight.

There are a number of circumstances under which you might bivouac:

1. *Planned*:
    (a) in preference to a crowded hut;
    (b) in preference to an expensive hut;
    (c) on a long route which is likely to take more than a day;
    (d) simply because you are enjoying yourself so enormously that you want to prolong the pleasure.
2. *Unplanned*: because you are
    (a) lost;
    (b) slower than anticipated;
    (c) overtaken by a storm;
    (d) involved in an accident.

The second 'unplanned' category can be catered for by making a habit of carrying a large polythene bag, big enough to accom-

Fig 175   Tim Jepson lighting the stove at a commodious bivouac on the Glacier Noir in the Dauphiné Alps. It is not every bivouac that allows you to spread your gear so far and wide.

modate a body – therefore it becomes a body. A bag big enough to house two is preferred by some. A slice of karrimat, that otherwise lives in your rucksack as a softener of sharp corners between load and back, will make a cold backside warmer, hard ground less hard, and a long night shorter, and all for a few ounces. Gloves, balaclava and a spare pullover, items which ought really to live in your sack too when not worn, will all sweeten the night.

If you are a sybarite or have the pocket for it you can invest in a Gore-tex bivouac bag, one each, or even in a small bivouac tent – either of your own design or one of a number of models on the market. A poly bag, however, will do to begin, certainly on the average first-season alpine routes.

Planned Bivouacs

Whether you plan to bivouac merely to avoid staying at a hut, for whatever reason, or because your intended route is likely or certain to demand one or more, the gear that you carry will be much the same. In any case, it is a balance between weight and comfort, distilled by experience. Such gear might include, in addition to a bivouac bag:

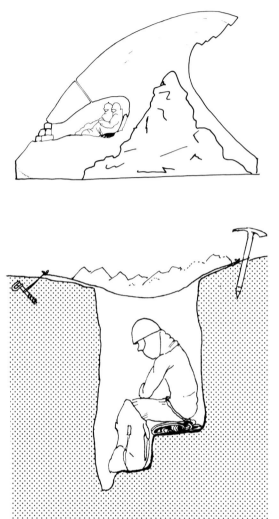

Opinions differ: some prefer a duvet because they say that you can snooze and climb in one. Others say that a duvet keeps only the top half of the body warm, seldom affords a good night's kip, yet causes the climber to be overheated in minutes if he tries to climb with one on. A sleeping bag, they will argue, need be no heavier (about 2lb) and much warmer. 'You pays your money (a fair bit of it in this case) and takes your choice.'

Some things worth considering in the selection of a bivouac site are:

1. Protection from falling stones, snow or ice. An overhang makes a fine roof.
2. Nearby water saves having to melt snow.
3. When you know you are to bivouac, select a good site before nightfall, rather than pressing on into the dusk and having to settle for a bad site for the sake of a few hundred feet climbed.
4. Avoid ridges if possible. They will be draughty and exposed to lightning.
5. Pick as flat a spot as you can, and make it flatter by removing offending stones. Secure yourself to the mountain if your ledge is small, or exposed (a rope will run from a harness through the neck of a sleeping bag to an anchor easily enough). Secure all your equipment too, especially boots, which should be tucked under the body if possible to keep them from freezing or, if they are fairly dry, taken into your bag with you for the same reason. Plastic boots don't freeze, of course, so there is no need to spoil them so. The inners might usefully sleep with you though, then they'll be pleasantly warm come the morning.
6. Water, melted or drawn the night before, will freeze overnight (as will water sources) if not stored in a bottle and slept

Fig 176   Snowholes can be dug wherever there is sufficient depth of snow.

1. Sleeping mat, ½ – ¾, or full body length.
2. Cooking pot and (a luxury) a mug and spoon.
3. Stove and fuel and lighter.
4. Duvet/sleeping bag (*see* below).
5. Some food/drink.

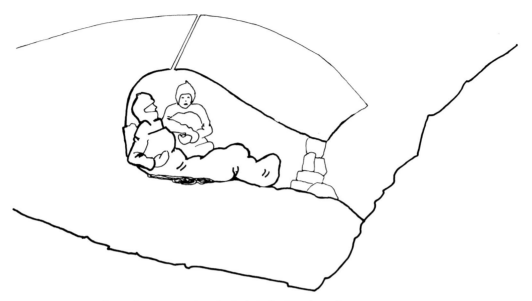

Fig 177   Try to have the sleeping bench slightly higher than the entrance so that you are lying in warmer air, and consider a ventilation shaft, unless you prefer a good fug.

with. Ensure the bottle is leakproof, and that the top is tight. Water frozen to ice in a pan will still produce water the next morning faster than melting snow.

7.   If you are on a snow slope it is fairly easy to cut a ledge on which to bivouac. Make the floor as smooth as you can and if possible inward sloping. An outward sloping floor is difficult to sleep on with an easy mind, even if you are belayed to screws or axes. Make the ledge big enough to lie down if you can, a good slumber is worth an extra half-hour's work.

Not all your bivouacs, planned or unplanned, will occur on exiguous ledges on awesome faces. Some will be on roomy buttresses, others on expanses of broken, easy ground, still others on perfectly flat snow. Use whatever nature has supplied and improve on it where possible. Here are some ideas for improvisation whether for a bivouac that was planned or unplanned or one that was brought on by an emergency.

6 That Very First Alpine Route

The next step, the best step – and not before time – is the route itself. Let's take a look, stage by stage, at that very first alpine route of that very first alpine season; a great time, a great moment.

You have elected to spend that first season in the Dauphiné – a wise choice, the Dauphiné (or Massif Des Ecrins) being one of the best of all the European alpine areas, blessed with a claimed (and as far as I can tell from the evidence of many sunblessed seasons, an actual) 300 days of sunshine a year, stunning scenery and a fine selection of alpine peaks with rock and ice and mixed routes at all grades, and especially at the first season end of the scale. Of the possible bases you have chosen the hamlet of Ailefroide, again a sound choice – spacious, indeed enormous, campsite, good showers, adequate toilet provision, some shops and restaurants, a river, boulders for bouldering and a 250m crag for 'resting' away those rest days: in all a setting as near to perfect as any to be found in the European Alps. (Ailefroide lies at the head of the Vallouise (or Gyronde) valley at 1500m. It may be reached from Argentiére la Bessée via the town of Vallouise by bus or car. Argentieré la Bessée is connected by rail to Grenoble.)

Driving up from Argentiére you could either check-in as you pass the campsite office, or you may have found yourself a space for your tent that you fancied, so you could set up camp there and then. By next morning a campsite attendant will have spotted the newcomers and a message will be tagged to your tent inviting you to register at the office. Campsite fees vary from region to region, but they are usually based on numbers of tents and cars to a party.

Since this is your debut you're dead keen; you stay off the beer that night (or ignore the hangover if you didn't) and by breakfast the next day you're poring over the guidebook in search of that first route. Your mate is equally keen but wishes to know what the weather forecast is before making his decision about which route, and wanders off to the Bureau des Guides to see what has been posted, returning in ten minutes with good news and predicted 'trés beau temps'.

Brews of tea follow brews of tea while the guidebook is thumbed and flicked and turned, and the map (bought locally or in Britain) consulted, measured and related to the descriptions from the book. A picture, a feel, for the area is developing. It may also be that you have acquired, or a friendly aunt has provided, or you have otherwise access to a copy of 'Rebuffat's One Hundred Best Routes in the Massif des Ecrins' and an illustration therein fires your imagination with technicoloured fancy. But whomever or whatever the arbiter, a choice is made: the Barre des Ecrins by the north-east ridge. Sound choice again; long and fairly high for a first route, but technically straightforward. Less fit, or more cautious teams might have opted for a lower peak and one with a shorter approach – but you are young and as we have said, keen. The guidebook (*Ecrins Massif: Selected Climbs*, John Brailsford, Alpine Club Guide Books, 1987) has this to say:

'North East Ridge

'From the N Couloir of the Barre Noire (or the ordinary route), traverse to the large snow boss forming the end of the NE ridge closest to the Barre des Ecrins.

'Climb steeply up the left flank of the boss and reach the ridge by an open, shallow gully slightly to the right of the lower section of the ridge and a steep but short step between 3,950m and 4,000m. Follow the snow crest to the foot of the step, traverse right on to the N face and climb the second rock chimney which you encouter (grade III, verglas). Reach the ridge following steep rock and then the crest of the ridge to the summit.

'Seasonal variations in conditions may increase the difficulties of the ridge by as much as two standards to D (normal time; 2 hrs from the boss to the summit).'

It will be seen from this description (and the photograph) that the route begins some way

Fig 178   The Northern aspect of the Barre Des Ecrins. The Barre Noire Couloir runs up the right side of the black rock triangle on the left of the picture (see also Fig 179). The NE Ridge is the one leading from the summit down to the left − to the top of the Barre Noire Couloir and towards the camera. The descent route (and voie normale *in ascent) zigzags up the immense snow slope behind the lower climber.*

up the mountain and is reached from one of two other routes, the North Face (or ordinary route and nowhere near as ferocious as the name or aspect suggest) or by the Barre Noire North Couloir. These descriptions now capture your attention.

'North Face

A.W. Moore, H. Walker, E. Whymper, C. Almer and M. Croz.
25 June, 1864
'A magnificent route without special difficulty, very popular. A fine view. The state of the glacier varies according to the year. The rimaye at the foot of the Brèche Lory can pose serious difficulties.

'From the Ecrins hut descend on to the Glacier Blanc by rocks facing the Ecrins. Follow the left bank of the glacier almost to the Col des Ecrins (1hr). Make your way towards the north slopes of the Barre, generally crossing an avalanche path. Go by snow slopes in the less-crevassed area of the glacier, contouring the rock rognon which supports the lower seracs, by the right (leaving on the right the seracs situated next to the Pointe de Bonne Pierre (serac fall danger)). Go towards the snow boss which forms the extremity of the NE arête of the Ecrins, [which is where we join our intended NE ridge. Reading on gives our intended line descent], and when the slope is less steep go obliquely right. When there is new snow go slightly left, cross a rimaye and the steep slopes and then slight right on the upper plateau of the glacier. Cross it, at the beginning under the final slopes of the Barre, until at the foot of the Brèche Lory which markes the extremity of the W arête of the Ecrins. Cross the rimaye a little to the right of the brèche (sometimes difficult) and climb to the brèche (1½ – 2 hrs). The brèche

is dominated by a step which cannot be climbed directly. Go along the base of the rocks to the left and climb a short chimney which leads 10m higher to a ledge. From there, climb obliquely left by easy rocks passing under this step. Join the crest of the W arête and follow it directly by its edge or a few meters from it by rocks and some snow slopes. The first ascent partly climbed to the ridge from a point some way short of the Brèche Lory and this line is often followed today if the rimaye can be crossed. Climb up to and past the Pic Lory and finally the summit (1hr: from the hut 3½ – 4hrs). Descend by the same route.

'La Barre Noire, North Couloir

F. Picard and G. Singer, 1954
'This variation to the normal route from the Glacier Blanc provides an excellent alternative means of ascent to the summit of the mountain. The route follows a wide, open, couloir and is often frequented nowadays by guided parties. It is safe from objective dangers. The couloir, followed by the ascent of the Barre des Ecrins by the NE ridge is highly recommended and is an airy and less frequented route than the Voie Normale. Grade of the NE ridge: PD + .

'From the Ecrins hut, follow the route towards the Col des Ecrins (Route No. 57). At a point opposite the North Couloir, cross the glacier. Climb the rimaye on the left, a few metres from the boundary rocks of the right bank of the couloir.

'Climb directly towards the col. At about two-thirds height, the angle steepens to around 50 degrees; trend rightwards for the final three or four rope-lenghts to leave the couloir adjacent to the rocky rib which bounds the left bank (2–3 hrs: 4hrs from the hut). Traverse right to join the normal

Barre Noire Couloir

From hut or bivouac

Fig 179   The Barre Noir Couloir as seen from head-on − an aspect which always makes alpine couloirs look considerably steeper than they really are. Look carefully at the top third of the couloir and you'll spot up to seven climbers, with another group at the col above, the first step of their route complete. Note the avalanche cone and debris, triggered by serac collapse on the N. Face of the Barre Des Ecrins. This photograph was marked to show a pal the way one summer.

175

route or follow the NE ridge to the summit.'

Other inter-relating factors that you might consider or study if you can rein in your enthusiasm for long enough are:

1. Food – for the hut and hill.
2. Equipment.
3. Route to the hut, length of walk.
4. Time of departure from campsite.
5. Whether to stay in hut or bivouac – which will effect point 2 and perhaps points 1, 3 and 4.
6. Overall conditions – glacier and mountain.
7. Weather forecast.
8. Descent.

But, although you'll get around to all these things, though not necessarily in that order – not that the order matters much – you're still engrossed with joys of the route and any extra thrills you can squeeze into this your first foray.

The word is that snow conditions are good. After a few minutes thought you decide since you are fairly adept ice climbers and expect to be able to deal with the couloir in short order, saving perhaps even an hour from the advertised time, to approach the Barre des Ecrins NE Ridge via the Barre Noire North Couloir. In any case the couloir demands only an ice screw or two and perhaps a second axe more than the North Face and you consider that to be a fair investment, at least as far as the hut from where you can spy out the land for yourselves and maybe change your minds at little cost beyond the energy expanded in the transport of that extra gear thus far.

Wise virgins, so far: giving some thought to equipment you settle for the list on page 65, augmented by that second ice axe (or hammer) and a couple of ice screws (or snargs or similar) each.

Now for the approach to the hut. Your map shows the way clearly: a drive (or hitch or walk to the end of the road at Le Pré de Madame Carle or Cezanne) and then a zig-zag climb up a well-trodden and picturesque path to the Refuge du Glacier Blanc at 2,550m – a height gain of about 650m and a leisurely, sunblessed, two hour stroll. From the refuge the path continues up and along the left bank (that is left taken from the direction of flow) of the Glacier Blanc, to the Refuge des Ecrins at 3,170m, a distance of 3½km, the last couple of which look as if they might involve the occasional foray on to the glacier itself. You reckon about 4–4½ hours for the complete walk and figure that because you'd like to arrive no later than 6 p.m. in order to give yourself time to relax, eat and get organised for the next day's great day, then you should think about leaving the campsite somewhere around 1.30p.m.

Then, browsing through the remainder of the guidebook, one of you spots a heading 'Huts' and reading on, discovers:

'Access to all the huts useful to the expeditions in this guidebook are by well used, clearly marked tracks. The Aigle hut is an exception, where the Tabuchet glacier and other detail complicates the route. The 1:25,000 maps recommended clearly indicate the position, and the winter and summer approaches for each hut. The following list indicates the capacity and responsible agencies only.'

And a little further along:

'Ecrins Hut. 3170m. This is owned by CAF

(Briancon) and was originally called the Caron Hut. Room for 120 guarded throughout the summer season, it often packs in 200 or more alpinists and visitors. It is wise to avoid the hut between the end of July and the middle of August unless one has booked via the Bureau des Guides in Ailefroide or Syndicat d'Initiative in La Berarde. Parties and large groups are strongly urged to take this precaution. Bivouac sites are sparse.'

It is the first week in August. You fear that the hut will be packed out. You ponder whether or not to bivouac. At last you decide that you'd rather commune with nature than 200 plus Euro-citizens, though the price of your solitude is a slightly heavier load – a light sleeping bag, sleeping mat, and a mug and spoon each; and between you a stove, pot and some food. You reason, though, that the slightly heavier load is a burden only as far as the bivouac site, for since you will be returning by the same way later on the morrow you can stash all the gear used in bivouac under a rock, take the route in light order, and pick up the remainder on the way home. Not bad reasoning. Geography is not always so helpful though, and often preferring a bivouac to a hut means carrying the bivouac gear on the route – making the bivouac a less attractive (and impractical) proposition than the case under discussion. Nevertheless a few huts are so crowded that some consider a bivouac to ' be the answer, despite the weight penalty, even sometimes, whatever the weight penalty.

It's approaching midday. Time for a brew and lunch. Then a careful pack ensuring that nothing has been forgotten. One of you has newish boots and is worried that his feet may blister before the hut. He wisely decides to pad up in a comfy pair of trainers

with boots secured atop his sack. (Some prefer always to approach in this way, even when boots are well worn). In this case those trainers can be left with the bivouac gear.

At Le Pré de Madame Carle you take the signposted path and begin the leisurely stroll amid a throng of daytrippers making their way up to or down from the Glacier Blanc Hut – though their Sunday day out may only be as far as the snout of the Glacier Blanc there to gambol, play, laze, admire or photograph.

Take it steady on your stroll, a rest at the Glacier Blanc hut will come soon enough. Enjoy the scenery, mountain architectural, human anatomical. By the time you reach the Glacier Blanc hut you'll have found your rhythm and should be comfortable enough to drink in the stunning views on all sides, but particularly over your left shoulder where the great North Walls of the Pelvoux and Pic Sans Nom lurk. You'll want water too – it can be thirsty work, those hut walks. There's ample water around though and any from streams will be good to drink – but avoid that from puddles, it may be polluted or just stagnant. Drink in plenty – dehydration is very debilitating. It may be that you are strolling in shorts; breeches, tracksuit or other climbing apparel having been stowed in your sack. This is a sensible arrangement on warm days, but be prepared to don more clothing as you gain height.

You rest at the hut maybe twenty minutes; time for a drink (a soft one or even a beer from the hut if you're well heeled), a photograph and a bask in wonderful alpine ambience. Then up and on again, toward the Ecrins hut – a less populated path by now. The path follows the lateral moraine (Left Bank) of the glacier which is falling steeply at this point and is, as a result, spectacularly crevassed. Safe on the apex of the moraine you can afford to enjoy the spectacle. In an hour or so the glacier flattens as you gain its crest and although the path continues to follow the moraine bank, annual and seasonal variations mean the occasional foray on to the ice itself. When this happens the way will be clearly shown by a trough gouged by the passage of thousands of feet: few of the owners of those feet will have roped up, and you too will probably decide not to bother – but if you are in any doubt, ignore the general trend, and follow discretion's hint.

Now you are amongst high mountains, the air is fine and fresh, the scenery grand: a good place to be. The walking is easy too, a gentle, steady rise for 1½ km. Ahead is the bulk of the Barre des Ecrins; northern aspect and most of your tomorrow, the up and down, in clear view: an exciting prospect.

The hut is close now, but we're bivouacking remember, so it's time to scout about for a spot with some dry rocks and a handy trickle of water. There are a good few about (the guidebook's warning notwithstanding) and even if it means stopping a few hundred metres short of the hut that is small distance to be covered in pre-dawn cool on the next day. In fact a bivouac site down level with the glacier will actually save you that last little flog up to the hut which sits 100m above it.

Now you can relax, and brew and eat at your leisure – and all with that wonderful backdrop. You can spy out the way tomorrow too, the reconnaissance conducted from your bivouac site, such is the panorama it commands. That is not always the case: sometimes considerable excursions have to be undertaken from hut or bivouac in order to recce the way from sleeping place to beginning of route.

From your bivouac the snow of the couloir looks good – white and fairly plentiful, with a happy absence of dark grey and black, the colour of old, iron-hard, unfriendly ice. It might look a touch steeper than you'd anticipated; alpine snow and ice routes have a habit of presenting a formidable aspect, head on. For a true perspective you need to look from the side. Then the angle can be disappointing.

Flatten an area to sleep on, lay down mat, fluff-up bag and toast in the multiple warmths of *alpengloh* and a brew, supper and a cosy spot (supper is soup, *flute* and a big brew; and then another).

Before settling in for the night, tidy up your area, particularly the kitchen. Check that stove and pot are to hand – breakfast will be taken long before the dawn. Know where the matches or lighter and headtorch are and anything else you are likely to need during the night or first thing next day. Stow anything that is not going to be needed immediately in your rucksack and keep that nearby. If your boots are wet (you may not have worn trainers) consider wrapping them in a poly bag and taking them to bed to keep them from freezing. Or, if your boots are plastic and the inners are damp, do the same with the inners – or wear them dry. Damp socks can be placed between vest and shirt, or shirt and pullover. It is better not to leave wet socks on the feet where they will come into direct contact with the inside of your sleeping bag and dampen the filling, reducing the bag's effectiveness – though this may be a small thing if only one bivouac is contemplated before a return to the valley. And sleep.

Set your alarm, or watch, or by some other means ensure a 2.30 reveille. That's one advantage of staying at a hut – you'll be woken at 2.30 a.m., if not before, whether you want it or not! At the appointed hour rise, or at least emerge sufficiently from your bag to get the brew on. Being prudent lads you'll either have taken your water bottles to bed so that they're not frozen (alpine beds can get pretty crowded) or at least filled a billy with water the night before – because yesterday's stream will have shrunk to nothing and will not flow again until mid-morning, by which time you'll be long gone.

With a bit of practice you'll judge your rising to perfection so that the moment you're fully booted and gaitered the water boils and tea or coffee quickly follow. If it is particularly cold, or you have time in hand, you may afford yourself the luxury of breakfast in bed, leaving the girding of loins and legs till later.

Concurrent activity is the key, packing, donning, fitting, stowing, girding, drinking – all at once. You're leaving all the bivouac gear behind, remember, so stow that safely out of sight – thefts even amongst the mountains are not unknown – and protected by a poly or bivouac bag. Keep the rope handy, you'll be needing that almost straight away, and don your harness now, to save fumbling around in five minute's time. Keep an axe out too – and while you're about it you could put on a helmet rather than wait until you're at the foot of the route, though that is an alternative. The weather promises to be perfect: stars shine bright in a cloudless sky – maybe a moon too – while it is still and cold. There's no decision to be made. It's on.

By now the dots of headlights will be punctuating the darkness as parties leave the Ecrins hut bound for the North Face, the *voie normale* and the route of your descent. As the minutes pass the dots lengthen to dashes and then by 4.30, a near continuous line as up to 200 climbers debouche on to the glacier, most of them bound for the same north face or at least as far as the Dôme de Neige. This is a bump along the way just tangential to the 4,000m contour, a height which holds a strange fascination for continental alpinists so that many, having gained the Dôme, but 86m short of a far finer true summit, that of the Barre des Ecrins itself, turn, satisfied, and head for home. Strange game, alpinism.

By the light of a headtorch and no later than 4.30 a.m., descend to the glacier, probably no more than a few feet, rope up (*see page 119*) and set off along the line of those dots – the path will be deeply trodden – until opposite the Barre Noire Couloir. Now cut across the glacier to the foot of it, where you are likely to be stopped by a rimaye. Climbers often set off from a bivouac wearing lots of clothes and then, fairly quickly, overheat. If this happens it's worth stopping to shed some clothing and to ventilate – overheating causes discomfort and wastes precious liquid, which will have to be replaced at some stage.

You should have gained the rimaye by 3.45 a.m. A brief stop, maybe a sip of water or juice, then rig the rope and gear for climbing, on with helmet if you're not already wearing it, and away with the leader of his first ever alpine pitch, on his first ever alpine route... etc. Depending on conditions and ability you might pitch the entire couloir's length, or you may move together the whole way, or a bit of both. Certainly the angle steepens at about two-thirds height and even if you have moved together thus far you may now begin to move in pitches, belaying on screws and axes before moving right to the finish. A competent team in reasonable conditions will reach the top of the couloir in two hours from the rimaye (6.30, on our schedule). Dawn, a wonderful alpine dawn, will have overtaken you somewhere in the couloir. Now you might allow yourself a drink and chunk of chocolate as you shorten the rope and prepare, after pitching, to move together up the NE Ridge. It'll be worth carrying the cameras at the ready too; the scenery is superb.

It is likely that you will dispense with most of the ridge moving together, though the occasional step may have you pitching again, and employing a selection of those belays shown on pages 150–156, especially in adverse conditions. The last of the ridge before the summit is wonderfully airy; a grand first route. By 8.30, no later than 9.30, you'll be on top, not just of your first alp, not just the Barre des Ecrins but of the whole of the Dauphiné range too – and, as far as you're concerned, the whole, wide world. You can now relax and feast your eyes on the panorama: Les Bans, the Meije, Pelvoux, Ailefroide – and a dozen more; mountains to feed dreams.

When you have feasted and rested (and drunk and eaten, or at least nibbled) prepare to descend, which in this case is to continue along the ridge for another 200m, again moving together, until a descent on to the glacier can be made. It is possible to scramble down here though some prefer to abseil, especially if the rimaye looks difficult. If abseil you prefer, arrange the ropes as described on page 163. An anchor advertised by a dozen old slings will show the start – and abseil in one rope's length to the glacier below. From here the way is stratight-forward though not entirely without danger: the glacier is crevassed – so better to stay roped; and seracs threaten parts of the path – so be prepared to move quickly

in places. At times you'll be sorely tempted into a bum-slide. If the way ahead is clear and obviously uncrevassed, and if the run-out is visible, and there is no dead ground, then it is a temptation that need not necessarily be resisted. But slide with caution and stay roped together. By the time you regain the Glacier Blanc it will be very warm and you'll be attending to thirst, and suncream, and maybe, again, to ventilation. Soon you'll be back at your gear stash where you can brew, relax, sunbathe and allow yourself a great beam of satisfaction.

It may be that you intend to remain in the area for another route tomorrow, in which case you have all afternoon to relax in, or you may be headed for the valley, a celebratory beer and a short rest, in which case you have all afternoon to do that in too. Whatever is the next step nothing can diminish that first big step that took in its stride that first route. If descend you do though, take care across the afternoon glacier – it would be a pity to delay that beer. (And don't forget, leave no trace of your bivouac: 'take nothing but pictures; leaving nothing but footprints'.)

Although every alpine route is unique, most will follow this general pattern. Variations might be: an approach to a hut by, or in part by, *télépherique* (cable car); a pure rock route where crampons and axe are dispensed with; a beginning from, and returning to, a hut; or a route of longer duration, perhaps as many as six days. But whatever later variations you encounter, and no matter what greater adventures come your way, nor despite later and higher hills, I'm prepared to bet that you never forget the first route.

An afterthought: It is unlikely that any-

Fig 180   'The population on the descent': a crowd makes its way back from the Ecrins and Dome de Neige summits. The zigs and zags of the way up and the 'direct' of the way down are easily discernible.

thing could have diminished that wonderous frisson of a first summit won or of that vista as 'Alps o'er alps arise' to the last horizon. But if diminishment there was it would have as likely been caused by the population on the descent – the *voie normale* in ascent remember, and this is the highest summit in the Massif and a popular 4,000m peak into the bargain. So if the crowds have rubbed some of the gloss off your day you might have vowed to avoid them next time out. This is usually possible.

The most popular routes in an area are often the best, the classics – and this is especially true at the easy end of the scale. It is not always the case, however, and even if it is it doesn't mean that the most popular route is the only good route thereabouts. Sniff about, you can usually nose out some solitude and the guidebook will often give opinions on what are good, enjoyable routes

– though even the guidebook might forget to underline a classic. So be as adventurous as you like, there are a few bad routes in the big hills, and in that first season everything is likely to be an excitement, to be worthwhile.

An unfortunate consequence of crowded routes, or indeed of almost any density of humanity, is litter. Some routes in the European Alps are only infrequently signposted with it, others are dotted, a few are bestrewn. I'm reluctant to preach but it's almost as easy to put wrappers and tins back in sack or pocket as it is to discard those things, and the reward is out of all proportion to the effort. Enough said, I hope. Conversely flowers and the like look better on the ground as they grow than in any hat, bosom or book. In fact it is against French law to pick alpine flowers – though that is a lesser concern than the damage such an act inflicts on the environment. Again, I hope, enough said.

7 Recent Trends and Variations

Things are changing in the European Alps. It's not that alpinism has changed: no, that game plays on much as before. Nor is it that the Alps themselves have changed – though in subtle environmental ways, or not so subtle, some would say – they have. Rather it is that the game that is now played in the Alps has changed. Changed to such an extent that in its most radical form it is no longer alpinism – which is indeed a curious thing to say in a place that gave the name to the alpine game in the first place. What has happened is that climbers have thrown the rock climbing game – ethics, attire, bolts and all – into the alpine arena, and well beyond the edge where it had long encroached; slap bang into the middle. And where the rock climbing game won't work, can't be played, won't be played, then the rules have been changed. So that the Dru is now a rock climber's playground – paradise; as is the Grand Capucin, the Pillar of Freney (scene of *the* alpine survival epic); and a dozen more once proud alps.

I think it is neither a good nor a bad thing: climbers accoutred in lycra tights, chalk, crag racks, sticky boots et al find a way of approaching the rock alp in trainers or by encasing their sticky boots in a specially designed outer, sturdy enough to bear crampons (and trainers can bear crampons in extremes). Once at the foot of the rock the mountain is treated as a crag for as far as it can be treated that way, or as far as the climbing is technically interesting – which is sometimes the top, the summit as

alpinists used to understand it – and often not. The West Face of the Dru, for example, is often climbed only as far as the shoulder (which in truth is quite a long way) when a retreat by abseil is sounded, all the way to the same bottom as we started from a few hours before. Where the rock game won't be played, where sticky boots won't stick, these routes end. Which is my only objection because that is often the best climbing; the difficult, technical, intricate, soul-searching, wild-eyed, staring mad, mixed stuff above and beyond.

The Pic Sans Nom – the Dauphiné one – is a good, or rather a bad example. This fine mountain has a north face *sans pareil*: remote, majestic, straight, true. The first half – about 1,500ft – is superb granite, a mighty wall of it, maybe 2,500ft wide; the second half some of the best mixed ground of the region. The whole makes a grand route – several grand routes actually; Alpinism par excellence; good rock followed by good mixed, topped by a summit, lone and mighty. Today the half of it makes rock routes. And this seems slightly daft because the Dauphiné region has acres of sunkissed roadside crags; because the N. Face of the Pic Sans Nom is remote, a lovely lonely place; and because, mostly because, a maze, a craze of bolts have been placed all over that good granite in order to make the rock game playable here. It seems to be as daft as marking out in white lines on that same granite a tennis court and calling whatever was then played on it tennis.

Fig 181   The 3,000ft North Face of the Pic Sans Nom.

There was no need: there are miles of rock better suited to the rock game. The N. Face of the Pic Sans Nom was created for the alpine game: and if proof is needed that it is an alp not a crag then go and count the bolts, every one of them saying that rock climbing doesn't suit this place. No matter. It's done. And won't be undone.

But there is much that's good come out of it all. Try skiing across to the Grand Capucin from the Torino Hut and changing from skis and snow to sticky boots and sunny spring SE facing rock and following that all the way to one of the most spectacular of all alpine summits before abseiling off – standard practice on that improbable needle anyhow – and skiing home all down the Vallée Blanche. This all strikes me as a perfect and economical blend of mountaineering skills; and nothing lost; plenty gained. Fun and fair. There are a hundred great routes on dozens of other mountains now climbed with this new freedom, products of this new imagination: on the Dru, the Aiguille de Blaitiére, the Requin, the Peigne, Pelerins and all. Nothing, or nothing much, lost in any of that. Plenty gained, as long as you accept the entire challenge, bottom to top.

But the game of alpinism has not died. It has found a new habitat – though it clings still to the Alps through traditionalists (who I think will always be a majority), on routes to which sticky boots won't stick (the majority again), on big new mixed routes (and there are still a few); on the great north faces; and in winter – of which a little more later. What has happened though, is that

Fig 182   Alpine rock: the south face of the Gletschorn (the Grauwand) in the Uri Alps of Switzerland. This sort of alp readily succumbs to the 'cragrat' approach – trainers, chalkbag, sticky boots and perhaps shorts for a south face. Research your approaches and descents, however, and check that they, as well as the route itself are indeed, 'cragratable'.

the game of alpinism has outgrown its birthplace as a son outgrown his parent's home, and has wandered far afield to the earth's last corners: to Alaska; to Norway; to Peru; to Patagonia; to the Arctic, the Antarctic; to New Zealand, to the Karakoram; to the Himalayas – even to the highest of them, to Everest. Alpinism thrives and glories in the trillion challenges left amongst that lot. So that, having served

your apprenticeship in Europe and having tired of the summer crowds, or of being overtaken by some lycra-clad gymnast on the first half of the route of your heart's desire as you cruise with a traditional flag at your masthead – then there's an entire world of alps elsewhere awaiting the first alpinist's hand or boot or front-point or axe. The rock game will pursue but never catch; there are too many places it can't follow.

There's a good alpine lesson in all this though: that old 'speed is a virtue' cliché. There's no faster way up the Bonatti Pillar than to shed all that traditional alpine paraphernalia and to go light, bright and sticky. And if it is fun – more fun – then why not? Why not indeed. Consider such an approach on any alpine route you are eyeing and if it will fit, if it will work then suit it, employ it.

WINTER ALPS

If, after a few seasons, you grow tired of the crowds on summer alps, or if you yearn for newer, greater challenges, then don't fret, empty alps and bigger challenges are just round the corner; or at least just round the season. Let autumn slip by and try an alpine winter, it's a bigger game altogether; harder to approach, colder, more to carry, longer to endure; bigger game, bigger struggle altogether. But the rewards of this greater investment are proportionately richer: empty mountains, space that need not be shared, lonely summits, intense satisfaction.

The differences between summer and winter alpinism will be apparent soon enough: two metres of snow on the roofs of houses and cars – and often on the hill too, though the wind may have blown it clear of ridges; temperature as low as − 30°C on

Fig 183   Climbing into the winter quarters of the Hornli Hut at the foot of the Matterhorn one January. Swiss law requires that some sections of all huts must be accessible throughout the winter. Other alpine nations usually have similar arrangements.

sunless north faces; thousands of skiers on tumultuous pistes and almost no one in a great silence beyond that: an entire mountain range to yourself and your partner.

Curiously there is an officially designated alpine winter: 21 December – 21 March, and those who regard that as the *only* winter apply the dates to all other mountains in the Northern Hemisphere. For Britons whose winters, year to year, vary wildly in span, intensity and even frequency, and who are in the habit of bagging an ice climb when they can get it, which to them defines winter whether it be October or May, such a procrustean definition of winter seems unnecessary. You are, of course, free to ignore it and climb your winter route on 20 December or 22 March. *Officially* it won't be recognised as a winter ascent, but since alpinism and officialdom seldom climb into the same bed, that might not worry you very much. (I hope not.)

Where are the winter routes? In theory any route that is climbed in summer is a potential winter route. In practice too. Sometimes easy summer snow routes will lie impossibly deep in snow giving a wade of a climb that is not much fun and very possibly one that is in danger of avalanching. A strong wind or week of sun, however, may transform that powder to névé so that a winter ascent is little more

Fig 184   The NE Face of Mont Blanc du Tacul (centre) and the NE Face Annexe in February. This face is the home of many fine and easily accessible winter climbs, particularly the gullies, most of which can be completed in a day, especially if approached on skis. AG is the line of the Albinoni/Gabarrou Couloir, a close-up of which is shown in Fig 5.

than a cooler version of the summer climb. Some north faces change from predominately rock climbs to first rate mixed routes, or even to predominately ice routes. Still other big summer rock routes remain rock routes, big cold winter ones. Even fairly easy rock can be difficult to climb on a cold day in big boots, big gloves and big sack — especially if it enjoys no sun.

ALPINISM IN THE GREATER RANGES

Alpinism travels well. Without modifi-

cation it will go most places. With the merest adjustment it will go anywhere, to the veriest summits of this planet, to the farthest horizons. That is alpinism's great joy. You can play it in ultra-civilised, over-civilised Zermatt on perfectly decent hardy annuals like the Matterhorn, road to railway to *télépherique* to signposted path to hut to summit via N. Face and all; or you can play it in remote Kishtwar via aeroplane, a railway (you'll never forget), a bus ride (you'll spend the rest of your life trying to forget), a memorable mule train to summits unseen, unrecorded, unknown via any route, face or facet you choose; or in frontier

Alaska from the foot of some mighty Arctic Alp, two plane rides from Heathrow and two days from your front door; or anywhere our earth has hurled its mountains at the sky.

WINTER GEAR

It's colder in winter so your gear must be warmer: top to toes. Plastic boots have made the task of looking after the toes much easier for they are much lighter than leather boots of equivalent warmth and with a thinsulite or alveolite inner are warmer than any predecessors – for no increase in weight over the summer version.

Inners can often be acquired separately so there is no need to buy a new pair of boots for winter climbing. Be sure they are not too tight though for tight boots or tight inners are the quickest way to cold feet. Once on an alpine winter climb I found that one foot was toasty warm, the other bitter cold. I recalled that in one boot – I couldn't remember which – I had an insole, the other I had lost somewhere along the way. I presumed that the cold foot wore the boot without the insole. Later the foot grew so cold and numb that I thought I'd better have a look at it and give it a rub before things became too bad. I took the boot off and to my surprise found the insole. It was the warm foot that had no insole – but what it did have was room, greater freedom to move, to wriggle and for the blood to circulate. The insoled foot was too tight by the thickness of that insole. The lesson was well learned – and obvious.

Most modern plastic boots will readily accept a variety of ski-mountaineering bindings and that is a very useful thing since the most convenient approach to many winter routes is by ski. It's a great way

home too! Snow shoes solve the same problem – but not so speedily or with quite the same *élan*. A supergaiter such as the Berghaus Yeti, or a thinsulite insulated Super Yeti completes the foot's ensemble, and adds insulation.

A reliable and efficient stove is a winter essential too if your expedition is to run longer than a single day – and most, perforce, will. Melting snow for water is a

Fig 185   Plastic boots, alveolite inners and supergaiters, a combination no heavier than traditional summer footwear and a good deal warmer. Some supergaiters, such as thinsulite lined Berghaus Super Yetis, are attached to the boot by means of a tight-fitting rubber rand. Other models rely on wire and straps. In the end it is best to stick them all at the boot welt with a contact adhesive – as has been done here. Then they'll stand a good chance of staying put for the winter season, and they can still be pulled off, intact, when summer comes round. The gaiters shown here are Carman Super-Gators (of the USA). They are cleverly lined about the foot with 3mm closed cell foam (like thin Karrimat), which provides ample insulation without obtrusive bulk.

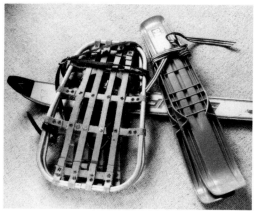

Fig 186 Some plastic boots readily fit many kinds of ski-touring bindings – those bindings with a front bail and crampon-type heel clip especially. Choose a boot with a pronounced welt at heel and toe so that it will accept step-in crampon bindings and crampon-type ski-bindings – such as the Salewa ski-binding shown here. Adding super-gaiters can interfere with the seating of either binding and you may have to trim slivers of rubber or canvass from heel and toe to accommodate the fastenings; a small sacrifice to convenience and warmth.

Fig 187 Over-snow mobility. Getting to and from winter routes can be a weary, waist-deep business. Skis, mini-skis and snowshoes may make the journey easier. Sometimes these implements can be left at the bottom of a climb to be collected on return, but if the way home doesn't pass that point then they have to be carried on the route – logistics to be considered at the planning stage.

tedious, but necessary, business, and the efficiency of ordinary gas and petrol stoves can be greatly improved by mounting them in a wind-shielding, heat-conserving container. This can be homemade by folding a sheet of tinfoil into a cylinder or, if you're a DIY handyman, by cobbling together something like the converted MSR shown in Fig 46 – in fact a clever combination of MSR and Trangia. An alternative is to buy a proprietary stove conversion supplied by a number of manufacturers.

Your clothing and sleeping bag too must be correspondingly warmer in winter. Give it a lot of thought. Combine layers and insulated garments – for legs and trunk – for warmth. Gore-tex or one of that family of fabrics, or Sympatex or one of that family, make an ideal shell. The head deserves a really thick balaclava and probably a hood too, while the hands will want inner gloves plus outer insulated mitts at the least. A spare pair of each on routes of any length is probably also essential. The sleeping bag should be the warmest you can afford.

The rest – and there's much more to winter alpinism – is experience and some summer alpinism first. Then you can walk as far on the wild side as you like, and the world, or all of it that is mountains – which is lots – is indeed your oyster.

Appendix I

FIRST AID

With any luck, and certainly with any judgement, you'll get through your alpine lifetime without needing to resort to first aid for anything more than a blister. But just in case, every party on the hills should carry a first aid pack containing:

1. Plaster (for blisters and small cuts).
2. Sterile wound dressing.
3. A roll of 3 inch elastic adhesive bandage (for strapping ankles, wrists, ribs, arm to side and one leg to the other).
4. Panadol or aspirin (for headaches and pain).
5. One or two triangular bandages.

Salt is a very useful commodity in mountains and may sometimes relieve cramp.

TREATMENT

Medical treatment is best left to a doctor or a skilled first aider, but it may sometimes be necessary for an unskilled person to give immediate first aid. Every mountaineer should learn at least the rudiments of first aid, and this can be done through the St John's Ambulance Association, the British Red Cross Society, in Scotland the St Andrew's Ambulance Association, or on special courses run at centres like Plas y Brenin, the National Centre for Mountain Activities.

These notes are a simple guide for the layman faced with a mountain accident.

General Principles

1. Check the airway for obstruction – mouth and throat. Check it frequently and keep it clear. *See* also Unconscious Patient, page 191.
2. Stop bleeding and apply dressing to open wounds.
3. Do not move the patient unless you are sure that there is no injury to the spine.
4. Treat for shock. Keep patient warm and relieve pain.
5. Immobilise broken limbs to relieve pain and to prevent further damage.
6. Do not experiment. When in doubt, do as little first aid as necessary since an unskilled person can do considerable damage by applying the wrong treatment.

Mountain Hypothermia

Mountain hypothermia or exposure is caused by the loss of body heat resulting from severe chilling, that is losing heat faster than the body is producing it, or exhaustion (most common in windy and wet conditions).

Signs and Symptons

1. Complaints of cold, tiredness or cramp.
2. Mental and physical lethargy. Lack of understanding of simple questions and directions.
3. Slurring of speech.
4. Irrational or violent behaviour.
5. Abnormality of vision.
6. Collapse and coma.

189

(These may not all be present, nor in the order given.)

All cases should be treated immediately, for mild cases can rapidly become very serious. If one member of the party suffers, keep a watch for others.

Prevention

(Refer also to sections on clothing, pacing, weather and accident procedures.)

1. Wear good clothing, including wind-proof and waterproof garments.
2. Avoid getting over-tired.
3. Do not go too long without energy-giving food and liquids.
4. If a member of the party is tired, cold and wet, seek shelter.

Treatment

Remove the causes:
1. Provide shelter. (*See* Emergency Bivouacs, page 168.) Use a tent or a large polythene bag. Give the patient prolonged rest.
2. Insulate from further heat loss – insulation from the cold ground is particularly important. Cover for head, face and neck is a great help.
3. Place the patient in a horizontal, or slightly head-down position and if possible, place a warm companion alongside him in a sleeping bag.
4. Warm food and warm sugary drinks are valuable if the patient is conscious, for example sugar, glucose, condensed milk.
5. Anxiety and stress is often an important contributory factor. Be cheerful and encouraging.
6. *Do not* rub the patient to restore circulation.

7. *Do not* allow further exertion; it will use up essential energy.
8. *Do not* give alcohol.

Frost-Bite

Watch for white noses and ears amongst your mates, and be aware of your own fingers and toes. Be prepared to remove a boot to inspect or to treat with body warmth.

Early or superficial frost-bite is best treated by applying body warmth or breathing on the cold part until sensation returns. The warmth of crutch or armpit, if possible, immersion in warm water, all work well. Once a frost-bitten part has been rewarmed, keep it warm. *Do not rub.* Treatment of deep or established frost-bite should be delayed until hospital treatment can be given. Protect the parts from rubbing or banging; the tissue will be devitalised and will readily tear.

Shock

Shock follows most accidents. The symptoms are pallor, weak and rapid pulse, cold, clammy skin, and a hunger for air. Make the patient comfortable and insulate from the cold ground. Reassure, allay anxiety and relieve pain. *Never* overheat a shocked patient.

Burns and Scalds

Cool the damaged part with cold water – immersing if possible. Use a non-adhesive dressing on the wound and treat the patient for pain and shock. Leave any adhering clothing on a burn. Remove hot wet clothing from a scald.

Cuts and Wounds

Cut away clothing to make sure there is no dangerous bleeding. Stop any bleeding by elevating the injured part and applying firm manual pressure over a firmly applied sterile dressing.

Sprained, Twisted or Dislocated Ankles

In general, do not remove the boot – it forms an excellent splint and sufficient relief from swelling can usually be obtained by loosening the laces.

Cramp

Massage the affected part and apply warmth. It may sometimes be relieved by drinking a salt soultion or eating a few grains of salt.

Unconscious Patient

Do not administer drinks or morphia. Make sure breathing is not obstructed and remove any dentures. Turn the patient on to his side in the recovery, or prone, position to prevent the tongue falling back and obstructing the airway, and to help the drainage of secretions.

Heat Exhaustion

Reduce temperature by moving into cool shade, use cold water (immersion if possible) and help perspiration by increasing air movement – fanning. Give salt in solution.

Fracture

Fractures must be immobilised before the patient is carried on a stretcher. If you have no experience or training in first aid, it is probably better not to try to immobilise a fracture unless it is causing the patient extreme pain. *Do not* try to straighten a broken limb.

Arm

Apply well-padded splints, such as a folded magazine or a rolled karrimat, to the fractured part. Rest an injured forearm in a sling and attach an injured upper arm to the chest. Elevate.

Leg

Use an ice-axe or stick to form a splint. Pad the splint and attach it to the injured leg. Pad well between knees and ankle, moving the uninjured limb to the injured limb and binding the legs together. Elevate.

Collar Bone

Place the hand near the other collar bone and bandage the whole shoulder and arm to the chest.

Spine

On no account move the patient. A spinal injury is often difficult to diagnose, but signs are pain in the back or numbness in the legs. If in the slightest doubt, treat as a spinal injury, and do not move until you have plenty of helpers and a proper stretcher.

Jaw

The patient may not be able to swallow or spit out saliva or blood. The head should, therefore, be inclined forward to allow these to dribble harmlessly from the mouth, rather than risk choking by lying the patient on his back.

Good mountain medical books are: *Mountaineering First Aid*, Mitchell; *Medicine for Mountaineering*, Wilkerson.

Appendix II

NOTES ON HELICOPTER RESCUES

Helicopters are widely used throughout the mountain world for rescuing victims of climbing accidents. These amazing and near ubiquitous machines have performed some incredible feats, plucking climbers from seemingly inaccessible places such as the White Spider on the North Face of the Eiger.

However, despite the impression given by these feats – which owe as much to the skill and daring of the pilot as to the performance of the aircraft – helicopters can't fly, or at least they can't land, any-where. And this should be borne in mind if you are a member of a party that is to be rescued by helicopter.

Some tips:

1. Make yourself as obvious as you can to the pilot by waving arms, using bright coloured clothing, generating smoke! (rarely practicable), flashing the sun off a shiny object or at night, a torch.
2. Pilots prefer to land or hover into wind. If you have any choice in the matter try to arrange things so that he can do this.
3. The average rescue helicopter (an Alouette MK III say) can land on about 20m diameter of flat land. Boulders, im-pending mountain-sides, trees and buildings all make landing more difficult and more hazardous.
4. On a restricted or sloping site helicop-ters can often touch down with one skid on – or hover just above terra firma. Beware

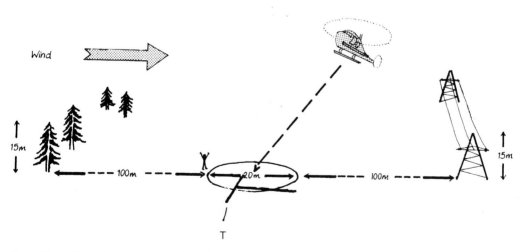

Fig 188   Place the 'T' so that the helicopter can land into the wind and give any obstacles as wide a berth as possible.

193

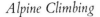
Approach

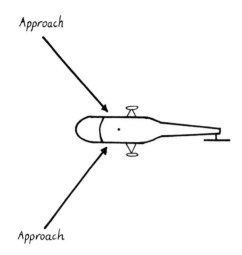

Approach

Fig 189   Always approach from a front quarter and always beware of the tail rotor.

the rotor blades in these circumstances – they will be much closer to the ground on the uphill side – sometimes perilously close.

5.   Even when a helicopter can't land a rescue can still be effected by using an on-board winch. Winches, however, are seldom more than 50m long.

6.   When landing, helicopters kick up their own local hurricane. Make sure that no unnecessary items are left lying around – sleeping bags, cooking pots, clothing – they may be blown into the rotors or sucked into an air intake. Rucksacks should be tethered or otherwise secured. Soft snow may have to be pre-trampled.

7.   Always approach a helicopter from the front, and preferably from the pilot's quar-

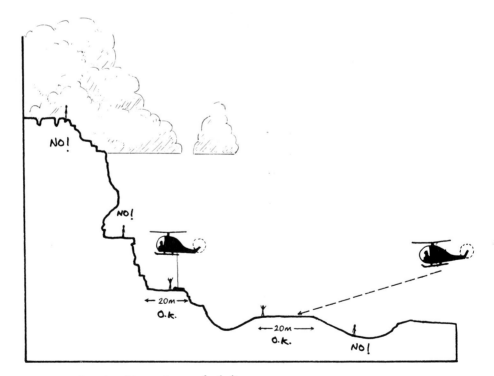

NO!

NO!

←20m→
O.k.

←20m→
O.k.   NO!

Fig 190   Typical 'go' and 'no go' areas for helicopters.

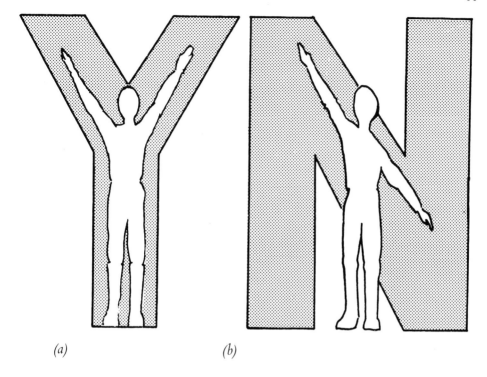

(a)   *(b)*

Fig 191   Signalling: (a) yes, I need help; (b) no, I'm OK.

ter. Beware rotors, the tail especially. On a slope approach from downhill of the front quarter. Heed the directions of pilot or crewman.

8.   Be prepared to move to a more accessible spot. This may mean lowering the victim from anchor to anchor on a figure of eight descendeur or friction belay plate or an Italian hitch.

Distress Signals

A sequence of six evenly spaced signals – whistles, torch flashes etc. – is recognised as an international signal of distress. Repeat after a gap of one minute and continue in this pattern. Some useful signals for aircraft are shown here. They may be marked out in snow with stones, clothing or by stamping – or anywhere else by using equipment – skis, rucksacks, clothing. Such signals should be at least 2½m high where possible.

1   require doctor, serious injury.
F   require food and water.
T   land here. The cross of the T should face into wind – as indicated in Fig 188.
LL   all's well.
SOS   International emergency signal.

Appendix III

ESSENTIAL KNOTS

I have introduced as few knots as possible; a practical minimum. They are, as shown in more detail in Figs 192–198.

1. Figure of eight
2. Prusik
3. Mariner's knot
4. Italian hitch
5. Clove hitch
6. Autoblock

Figure of Eight

This knot has two main uses. As shown in Fig 192, it is used for joining climbing rope to harness. As shown in Fig 193 it can be used on any occassion when a loop is needed in a rope: for belaying, in crevasse rescue, for tying on the middle man in ropes of more than two, or as a stopper knot – on the end of an abseil rope, for example.

To join climbing rope to a harness:

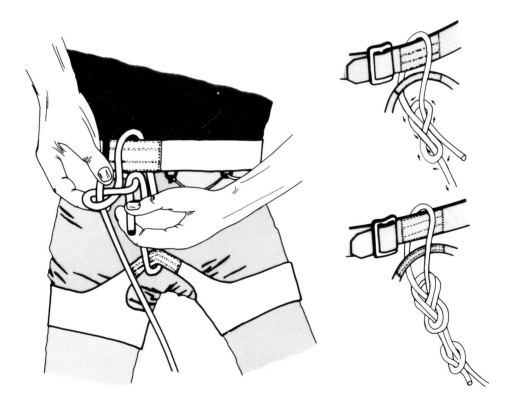

Fig 192   Figure of eight knot.

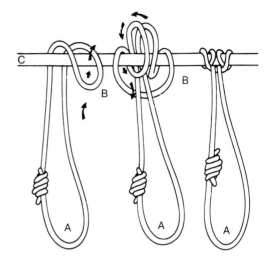

Fig 194   Prusik knot.

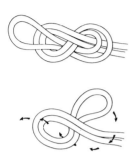

Fig 193   Figure of eight knot joining climbing rope to harness.

1.   Tie a single figure of eight in a single rope about 12 – 18in from the end, and thread that end through leg loop, connecting strap and waist belt (or other appropriate attachment point).

2.   Follow the first single figure of eight with the (shorter) end of the rope, as shown by the arrows.

3.   Snug up the resultant knot and complete with a half-hitch as insurance.

Note   The loop, or bight, encircling the leg loop, connecting strap and waist belt should be fairly snug. Too big a loop will allow the leg loop to droop uncomfortably at the front.

The Prusik Knot

This is perhaps the simplest of all the friction knots. Pass the longer end of the loop (A) through the shorter end (B), and then pass the longer end around the climbing rope (C) twice (longer end through shorter end both times). Pull tight and arrange the turns so that they lie flat and neat. If two turns do not provide sufficient friction, then you may add as many additional turns as are necessary. The diameter of the prusik cord must be smaller than that of the main rope: a soft 5mm prusik loop works best on 9mm climbing rope; a 7mm prusik is too big on a 9mm rope. If a prusik deforms in use it can fairly easily be thumbed back into shape.

The Mariner's Knot

This is used for connecting a rope to an anchor where it may be necessary later in the operation to release the rope when weighted. For the knot shown in Fig 195, the karabiner would be clipped in at A. The same end could be achieved with a simple sling, but then it would be difficult, perhaps impossible, to unclip under load. A simple but expensive solution would be to cut the tape. The mariner's knot saves cash and rescues those who have forgotten their

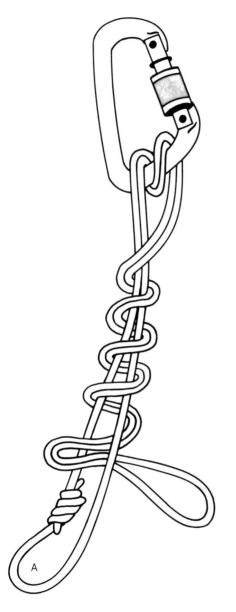

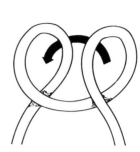

Fig 196   *Italian hitch.*

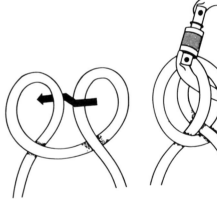

Fig 197   *Clove hitch.*

Italian Hitch

This is a wonderfully versatile friction hitch for belaying the live climbing rope, in direct or indirect belays. This hitch offers sufficient dynamic friction to allow the most serious falls to be held with comparative ease. Another handy feature is that the hitch is reversible. In Fig 196, A is the live rope and is being taken in by pulling down on B. This can be simply reversed by pulling down on A, with perhaps slight upward encouragement

Fig 195   *Mariner's knot.*

pocket knives. The arrows indicate the direction of pull. (For the application of this knot in crevasse rescue, *see* page 143.)

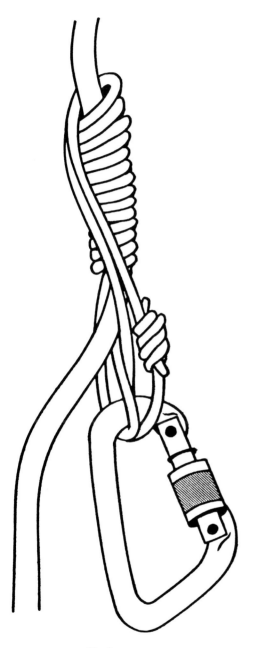

Fig 198   Autoblock.

at B, until the knot is reversed and the live rope at A is being paid out.

The hitch can also be used to abseil on, but this is not recommended because it results in a kinked rope. In all, it is an essential part of an alpinist's armoury.

Clove Hitch

These are quick, simple to tie, easy to adjust knots for belaying.

Shape two loops as shown in Fig 197, and pass the second *behind* the first. Clip the karabiner through both loops.

The Autoblock

The autoblock is a very useful friction knot. It is an invaluable component in crevasse rescue procedures because it applies friction without encouragement, so that it can be left to operate beyond the reach of a rescuer.

Take a loop of cord (such as prusik loop) and pass it around the climbing rope until all but the two ends have been consumed in the turns. Clip into those two ends with a karabiner and the knot is complete.

Some of you might ask why not use autoblocks on the rope instead of prusiks when travelling on glaciers, thereby saving the time and inconvenience of replacing at least one of those prusiks with an autoblock (*see* crevasse escape, page 134). The answer is that whilst the notion is fine in theory, in practice an autoblock travels badly, tending to unravel unless the ends are held jointly by karabiner – a task not easily performed by a team on the move. A prusik holds well on the move; an autoblock is better for autoblocking – horses for courses.

Appendix IV

GLOSSARY OF EUROPEAN ALPINE TERMS

Aiguille (French for needle.) A sharp-pointed mountain, particularly in the Mont Blanc range.

Arête A sharply defined ridge.

Bergschrund (Also called rimaye.) The crevasse separating the upper ice of a glacier from the mountain behind, often presenting the first serious obstacle of a route. Strictly speaking a bergschrund is between ice and ice; the crevasse separating glacier from the rock of a mountain is, again strictly speaking, a randkluft. In general usage, however, the British use the first word for both features.

Brèche Gap or notch (France).

Cirque A cwm or corrie – an enclosure of mountains.

Col A saddle or pass, usually between mountains.

Cornice A lip of snow or ice protruding from the crest of a ridge or arête, formed by snow being deposited by the wind. Big cornices may overhang the slope beneath the crest by many metres.

Couloir A gully of almost any height or width (or indeed, steepness).

Diedre An open corner, like that of a book opened at right angles.

Duvet A quilted down jacket.

Gendarme A prominent rock tower on a ridge.

Moraine Bank of stones and other debris deposited by a glacier.

Névé The upper reaches of a snow or ice field that feeds a glacier (also firn); or snow with a surface hardened by thaw/freeze action.

Randkluft The crevasse between the snow-field and the rock of a mountain – usually referred to, slightly inaccurately, as a bergschrund.

Rimaye *See* Bergschrund.

Rognon A large boulder or protruberance of rock (or terra firma) standing proud of the glacier.

Sastrugi Wave sculpting of snow by wind.

Serac A tower or pinnacle of ice, usually evident in ice falls or ice cliffs where a smaller mass is breaking off a larger.

Verglas A thin layer of ice coating rock.

Appendix V

ALPINE ASSOCIATIONS WORLD-WIDE

Andorra
Club Pirineng Andorra
Carrer de la Unio 2, 20
Andorra-la-Vella

Argentina
Federacion Argentina de Ski y Andismo
Viamonte 1560
1055 Buenos Aires

Austria
Verband Alpiner Vereine Osterreichs
Backerstrasse 16 (11)
1010 Wien 1

Osterreichischer Alpenverein
Wilhelm-Greil-Strasse 15
6010 Innsbruck

Belgium
Club Alpin Belge/Belgischer Alpen Club
Rue de l'Aurore 19
1050 Bruxelles

Bolivia
Club Andino Boliviano
Avenida 16 de Julio 1473
Casilla 1345
La Paz

Bulgaria
Fédération Bulgare D'Alpinisme
Boulevard Tolboukhine 18
Sofia 1

Canada
Alpine Club of Canada
P O Box 1026
Banff
Alberta TOL 0C0

Fédération Quebeçoise de la Montagne
1415 East Jarry Street
Montreal
Quebec H2E 2Z7

Chile
Federacion de Andinismo de Chile
Vicuna Mackenna 44
Casilia 2239
Santiago

China
Alpine Association, R O C
30 Lanchou St
Tapai
Taiwan

Czechoslovakia
Ceskoslovensky Horolezecky Svaz
Na Porici 12
11530 Praha 1

Denmark
Dansk Bjergklub
c/o N.O. Coops Olsen
Fuglesangvej 42
DK – 3460 Birkeroed

Ecuador
Association de Excursionismo Y Andinisno
de Pichincha
Casilla 8288
Officina de correo american y mazosca
Quito

Finland
Suomen Alppikerho
c/o Veikko Korhumaki
Juholankatu 110
04400 Jarvenpaa

France
Fédération Française de la Montagne
20 bis
Rue La Boetie
75008 Paris

Club Française
7 Rue La Boetie
75008 Paris

Germany
Deutscher Alpenverein
Praterinsel 5
8 München 22

Great Britain
Alpine Club Library
74 South Audley Street
London W1Y 5FF
Tel: 01 499 1542

British Mountaineering Council
Crawford House
Precinct Centre
Booth Street
Manchester
M13 9RZ

Expedition Advisory Centre
Royal Geographical Society
1 Kensington Gore
London
SW7 2AR
Tel: 01 581 2057

International Map Centre
12 – 14 Long Acre
London
WC2E 9LP
Tel: 01 836 1321

The National Centre for Mountaineering
Activities
Plas y Brenin
Capel Curig
Gwynedd
North Wales
LL24 OET
Tel: (06094) 363/214/280

Greece
Fédération Hellenique D'Alpinisme et de
Ski
Karageorgi Servias 7
Athenes 126

Guatemala
Federacion Nacional De Andinismo
Palacio de los Deportes
2° nivel zona 4
Guatemala City

Holland
Koninklijke Nederlandse Alpen
Vereniging
Lange Voorhout 16
2514 EE-s-Gravenhage

Hungary
Magyar Hegymaszo Klub
Bajscy Zsilinszky ut 31.11
1065 Budapest 6

India
Indian Mountaineering Foundation
Benito Juarez Road
New Delhi 110021

Iran
Iran Mountaineering Federation
PO Box 11 – 1642
Tehran
Islamic Republic of Iran

Ireland
Federation of Mountaineering Clubs of
    Ireland
Sorbonne 7
Ardilea Estate
Dublin 14

Israel
Club Alpin Israelien
PO Box 53
Ramat-Hasharon 47100

Italy
Club Alpino Italiano
Via Ugo Foscolo 3
20121 Milano

Federazione Italiana Sport Invernali
Via Piranesi 44
20137 Milano

Alpenverein Sudtirol
Serneisplatz 34/1
39100 Bolzano

Japan
Japanese Mountaineering Association
c/o Japan Amateur Sports Association
1 1-1 Jinnan
Shibuy-Ku
Tokyo 150

Korea
Korean Alpine Federation
29-1 Myoungryun-Dong 4GA
CPO Box 6528
Seoul

Korean Alpine Club
New Pagoda Building
Room 506
39, 2-Ga Jongro
Jongro-Ku
Seoul

Liechtenstein
Liechtenstein Alpenverein
FL 9496 Balzers

Luxembourg
Groupe Alpin Luxembourgeois
Place d'Armes 18
Boîte Postale 363
Luxembourg

Mexico
Federacion Mexicans de Excursionismo Y
    Montanismo
Eje Central Lazaro Cardenas 80
Desp. 408
Deleg Cuauhtemoc
08090
Mexico D.P.

Nepal
Nepal Mountaineering Association
16/53 Ran Shah Path
PO Box 1435
Kathmandu

New Zealand
New Zealand Alpine Club
PO Box 41–038
Eastbourne

Norway
Norsk Tindeklub
PO Boks 1727
Vika
Oslo 1

Pakistan
Alpine Club of Pakistan
228 Peshawar Road
Rawalpindi

Peru
Club Andiano Peruano
Casilla Postal 5360
Lima 18 (Miraflores)

Poland
Polski Zwiazek Alpinizmu
U1 Sienkiewicz 12/439
00–010 Warszawa

Portugal
Club Nacional de Montanhismo
Rue Formosa 303–2°
Porto

Spain
Federacion Espanola de Montanismo
Alberto Aguilera 3–4°
Madrid 15

Sweden
Svenska Klatterforbundet
PO Box 1245
75142 Uppsala

Switzerland
Club Alpin Suisse
Geschaftsstelle SAC
Helvetiaplatz 4
3005 Bern

Rendez-Vous Haute Montagne
Postfach 15
6390 Engelberg

Turkey
Turkiye Dagglik Federasyonu
Beden Terbiyesi Genel Mudurlugu
Ulius Ishani A Blok
Ankara

USA
American Alpine Club
113 East 90th Street
New York
NY 10028

USSR
Fédération D'Alpinisme D'URSS
Lushnetzkaja Kai 8
119270 Moskau

Yugoslavia
Planinarski Savez Jugoslavije
Dobrinjska 10/1
Beograd

Appendix VI

FURTHER READING

Tales, Adventure, Biographies

Barry, John *The Great Climbing Adventure* (1985), and *Snow and Ice Climbing* (1987)

Beckey, Fred *Mountains of North America* (1982)

Bonatti, Walter *On the Heights* (1964)

Bonington, Chris *I Chose to Climb* (1966)

Brown, Joe *The Hard Years* (1967)

Brown, T. Graham *Brenva* (1944)

Buhl, Hermann *Nanga Parbat Pilgrimage* (1956)

Cassin, Ricardo *Fifty Years of Alpinism* (1981)

Diemberger, Kurt *Summits and Secrets* (1971)

Gervasutti, Guisto *Gervasutti's Climbs* (1957,1978)

Gillman, Peter and Haston, Dougal *Eiger Direct* (1966)

Harrer, Heinrich *The White Spider* (1959)

Haston, Dougal *In High Places* (1973)

Jones, Chris *Climbing in North America* (1976)

Kor, Layton *Beyond the Vertical* (1983)

Lukan, Karl *The Alps and Alpinism* (1968)

Morse, Randy *The Mountains of Canada* (1978)

Mummery, A.F. *My Climbs in the Alps and the Caucasus* (1895)

Noyce, Wilfrid *The Alps* (1964)

Patey, Tom *One Man's Mountains* (1971)

Pause, Walter and Winkler, Jurgen *Extreme Alpine Book* (1979)

Perrin, Jim *Mirrors in the Cliffs* (1983)

Rebuffat, Gaston *Starlight and Storm* (1954)

Robson, Peter *Mountains of Kenya* (1971)

Roper, Steve and Steck, Allen *Fifty Classic Climbs of North America* (1982)

Shepherd, Nigel *Self Rescue Techniques for Climbers and Instructors (1987)*

Smythe, Franck *Climbs in the Canadian Rockies* (1951)

Stephen, Leslie *The Playground of Europe* (1871)

Terray, Lionel *The Conquistadors of the Useless* (1963)

Ward, Michael (ed.) *The Mountaineer's Companion* (1966)

Whillans, Don and Ormerod, Alec *Don Whillans. Portrait of a Mountaineer* (1971)

Whymper, Edward *Scrambles Amongst the Alps in the Years 1860–69* (1871)

Wilson, Ken (ed.) *The Games Climbers Play* (1978)

Winthrop Young, Geoffrey *On High Hills* (1934)

Text Books

Barton, Bob *A Chance in a Million: Scottish Avalanches*

Blackshaw, Alan *Mountaineering, From Hill Walking to Alpine Climbing* (1965)

BMC *Climbing Knots*

BMC *Safety on Mountains*

Clarke, Charles and Salkeld, Audrey *Lightweight Expeditions to the Great Ranges* (1984)

Cleare, John *Collins Guide to Mountains and Mountainering* (1979)

Cliff, Peter *Mountain Navigation*

Fawcett, Lowe, Nunn and Rouse *Climbing: A Climber's Handbook* (1981)

La Chapelle, Ed *The ABC of Avalanche Safety* (1961)

Langmuir, Eric *Mountaincraft*

Mountain magazine *World Climbing*, introduced by Terry King (1980)

Noyce, Wilfrid and McMorrin, Ian *World Atlas of Mountaineering* (1969)

Scott, Doug *Big Wall Climbing* (1974)

Medical

Hackett *Mountain Sickness*

Houston, Charles *Going High, the Story of Man and Altitude* (1980), and *Going Higher* (1984)

Mitchell *Mountaineering First Aid*

Wilkerson, James *Medicine for Mountaineering* (1967, revised 1985), and *Hypothermia and Frostbite*.

Index